Blueprint

for

Living

ENDORSEMENTS

The complexities of life today are complicated by a secular worldview that doesn't work. Therefore, it is no wonder people need help to successfully navigate and have victory over their hurts, habits, and hangups using a Biblical Worldview. *Blueprint for Living* goes a long way in providing an accurate and clear balance of Bible-based principles with practical insights to make living a new life in Christ filled with triumphs amid life's struggles. I suggest that this book be read and its Biblical principles be applied. Then, get another copy to pass along to others. You'll be glad you did!

—Dr. Stan Ponz,
President of Make It Clear Ministries and Clarity Christian College in San Antonio, TX BA, ThB, MDiv, DMin

Practical, authentic, and with a straightforward, no-nonsense approach, Cynthia Warrick shares insightful tips for believers to apply to their everyday lives in order to find wholeness. Readers are encouraged by examples and illustrations laid out in *Blueprint for Living*. Broken, weary, and discouraged, this book will remind anyone of God's grace and redemption as they search God's Word and, by His strength alone, seek to live it out.

—Dr. Monica Rose Brennan,
Associate Professor & Director of Women's Leadership, School of Divinity, Liberty University Department of Christian Leadership and Church Ministries

Cynthia Warrick has written a guide on how to love yourself and others with the heart of Christ. Ms. Warrick writes from years of experience in the world of Life Coaching/Counseling, and I treasure her insight and her practical advice on how to connect more deeply with people, oneself included, who urgently need to understand how much the Lord Jesus, the great physician, loves us. Prepare yourself for spiritual growth and scriptural healing.

—Anthony Cox, Former Adjunct Professor, University of AlabamaMember of Xchange Ministry at Hickory Grove Baptist Church

Blueprint

for

Living

10 BIBLICAL PRINCIPLES TO HEAL YOUR LIFE

CYNTHIA WARRICK

REACHOUT
PUBLISHING

ISBN: 978-1-998188-12-3 (Paperback)

ISBN: 978-1-998188-13-0 (Hardcover)

ISBN: 978-1-998188-14-7 (Ebook)

Available in paperback, hardcover, and e-book

the content of these sites and numbers for the life of this book.

Reachout Publishing
PO Box 159, Clyde, Alberta
T0G 0P0
www.reachloveconnect.com

TABLE OF CONTENTS

ACKNOWLEDGEMENTS

Behind every book, there's a story about the author: how they conceived the idea, developed it, and, most importantly, persevered to bring it all together. A difficult childhood marked my journey, but I had a great deal of help in writing this book. I am especially grateful to Jesus Christ for saving me and guiding me to know Him more each day.

To Jean Hartz Goddard, my girlfriend since the sixth grade. We had mutual faith and encouraged one another until she passed to be with the Lord. She was always my champion and encourager. We will laugh again in glory someday.

To Florida Bible College, which taught me God's word book-by-book and verse-by-verse. Through the Bible, I found the joy of my faith and was inspired to desire the abundant life I could have in Christ.

To my mother-in-law, Teri Ward, who shared much

laughter, loved my children, and made a remarkable impression on the lives of our whole family. She left a gigantic hole in our hearts.

To my children, Jason, Jessica, Scott, and Kevin Ward, who were an absolute delight to raise (most of the time) and continue to amaze me with everything they do.

To my former pastor, Rick Blackwood, who taught me how to truly love God's word. He is with Jesus now, but I'm certain he is reaping the blessings he sowed on earth.

To my friends, Chris and Bill Rivera, Beverly and Anthony Cox, and Mike and Noreen Shell, who exemplify the love Christians should have for each other.

Last but certainly not least, I thank my husband, Gib, who shows me every day that he loves me well.

"When you pass through the waters, I will be with you; and through the rivers, they shall not overwhelm you; when you walk through fire you shall not be burned, and the flame shall not consume you. For I am the Lord your God, the Holy One of Israel, your Savior."

—Isaiah 43:2–3 (ESV)

PREFACE

I have mused over this book for a long time. As a life coach/biblical counselor for about 30 years, I have come to realize that many Christians do not have any idea that the Bible is a blueprint for our lives. I came to Christ at about the age of six, yet by the time I was 17 and going to Bible college, I could probably only quote John 3:16. I thought most Christian kids were fakes—nobody could be that happy. There was a complete disconnect between the scriptures and how I conducted my life. I don't remember any churches I attended stressing the importance of reading the Bible or recall any instruction to think about the readings. Most importantly, we never learned to let God change our hearts and attitudes. We never learned to actually *Think* about what we were reading and allow God to change us.

How do you get the most out of the Bible? My husband figured out that if one reads two chapters in the Old Testament and two chapters in the New Testament daily, you will read the New Testament three times a year and the Old Testament once a year.

Forget what you have been taught, and while reading, think about what the Bible says. For instance, do you know the Bible never says Eve ate an apple? We don't know what kind of fruit it was, nor does it mention three wise men, only three gifts. You will be surprised how interesting it can be when you give God a chance.

When I started *really* reading the Bible, I began to see change. My attitude and my heart started to feel joy and peace. If you find it difficult to understand, turn to verse John 14:26 (ESV), "But the Helper, the Holy Spirit, whom the Father will send in my name, he will teach you all things, and bring to your remembrance all things that I said to you." In other words, once we accept Christ as our Savior the Holy Spirit lives within us and helps us understand the scriptures. All we must do is ask! It's an amazing truth that a lot of Christians don't know. You do not have to figure out the difficult scriptures. As they taught us in bible college, read the verse in the passage's context; that alone will help you in your understanding.

When my children were one, three, five, and seven (yes, you read that right), I often listened to a Christian help center on the radio called *The Meier Clinic*. As I listened to the callers' problems, I'd think of advice to give the callers. To my surprise, often, the advice given was the same as mine. Why? Because they were using the Word of God as the foundation.

It astounds me how many Christians do not have a foundation for their lives. It seems crazy to say that now because I've been one of those people. How soon we forget where we once were at the beginning of our journey with Christ. We often have short-term memories, which allows us to become judgmental of others. Remember, we are all on this journey together, each moving at our own pace and with individual life experiences.

It is my sincerest hope that this book will help you navigate life's challenges. Through my experience facilitating parenting classes, teaching in jails, creating a premarital program, and conducting group, couple, and individual therapy—including sexual abuse groups—I've realized just how many problems exist in the world. If everything was perfect, who would seek Christ? I once heard a saying I've never forgotten: "Many people fall to their knees when they are in trouble. It takes a true man (or woman) of God to prostrate themselves when things are going well." God promises life, but it is not an easy path. It is a daily commitment to set your mind on Christ and allow Him to change your life.

> "I am come that they might have life, and that they might have it more abundantly."
>
> —John 10:10b (KJV)

> "And be not conformed to this world: but be ye transformed by the renewing of your mind, that ye may prove what is that good, and acceptable, and perfect, will of God.
>
> —Romans 12:2 (KJV)

1

THE GOLDEN RULE

Blessed are those who hunger and
thirst for righteousness, for they
will be filled. Blessed are the merciful, for they will be shown mercy.

—Matthew 5:6–7 (CSB)

In the Sermon on the Mount, Jesus tries to get the
people to think differently about their relationship
with God. Prior to this sermon, the Jews saw their
relationship with God solely in terms of laws, rules,
and regulations. They believed that if they followed all
the external rules, their relationship with God would
be fine. In the Sermon on the Mount, Jesus wanted to
focus their attention on the internals. The law emphasized the externals; it was about washings, feasts, and
diets to maintain the purity of the flesh (Hebrews
9:13). However, Jesus emphasized the internals so
the people could have a clear conscience.

You see, Jesus wants us to stop justifying

and vindicating ourselves. He wants us to realize our behavior reflects on Him. As Matthew 5:11–12 (CSB) says, "You are blessed when they insult you and persecute you and falsely say every kind of evil against you because of me. Be glad and rejoice because your reward is great in heaven. For that is how they persecuted the prophets who were before you." When was the last time you rejoiced while being persecuted? I bet you don't have to think about it for long. It doesn't happen often since many of us never discuss our faith. If we are maligned because of our message and not our personality, we should know we are in good company. Jesus did nothing wrong and yet He was hated. (John 15:25)

Many Christians believe they are persecuted for their message when, in reality, they are rejected because of how they deliver it. In Matthew 5:13, we are called to be like salt. Often, the focus is on the preservative qualities of salt, but its primary use is to enhance the flavor of food. Likewise, as Christians, we should aim to be pleasant additives, enhancing and improving the lives of those around us.

Christians often want the unsaved to clean up their act before they come to Christ. We need to work on building relationships and loving the person like Christ instead of talking about their sin. We should explain and emphasize their need for a Savior. How can an unsaved person *clean up their act* without the Holy Spirit to guide them? Satan often distracts Christians by urging them to focus on fighting social injustice rather than emphasizing the importance of leading people to Christ, teaching them the Word, and allowing the Holy Spirit to transform their hearts.

The world should feel that we love them, and that Christians want to steer them toward Christ, who loves them beyond measure. I recall having lunch in the hospital break room when a political news story came on TV. One of my coworkers asked me what I thought, and I responded, "I believe in voting according to my convictions, but I don't let myself get overly worked up about it." The Bible says, "The king's heart *is* in the hand of the LORD, *Like* the rivers of water; He turns it wherever He wishes." (Proverbs 21:1, NKJV). My coworker replied, "That's probably the best statement I've heard; it totally makes sense." I then shared the gospel with her. Instead of talking about politics, I was able to answer her question by talking about Christ—season with salt. Be aware of what is happening in the world, and as I Peter

3:15 (NIV) states so clearly, "But in your hearts set apart Christ as Lord. Always be prepared to answer to everyone who asks you to give the reason for the hope that you have. But do this with gentleness and respect." Be the kind of person who draws others to Christ. We should enhance people's lives like salt to a stew, which in turn causes them to want to know more about the Christ who dwells within you and how He changed your life.

> "So in everything, do to others what you would have them do to you, for this sums up the Law and the Prophets."
>
> —Matthew 7:12 (NIV)

I often wonder why this is referred to as the Golden Rule? Perhaps it's because of the immense value—like gold, the highest standard—of showing respect and care for one another. This verse is often misquoted as "Treat others the way you are treated," which has a completely different meaning.

It is easy to reciprocate kindness to those who are kind to us. It doesn't require power from the Holy Spirit to do so. People of all religions and walks of life can do this. The hard part is being kind to people who are unkind to us. How do you show kindness to the unkind? The Holy Spirit dwells within you once you have trusted Christ as Savior. As Ephesians 1:13 (NKJV) says, "In Him you also *trusted*, after you heard the word of truth, the gospel of your salvation; in whom also, having believed, you were sealed with the Holy Spirit of promise." The real question is, how much does the Holy Spirit have of you? While we receive 100% of the Holy Spirit at salvation, the amount of mind and spirit He has of us fluctuates. It is extremely easy to pull away from the Lord and focus on doing what we want to do.

We don't have to be at someone's beck and call or allow others to step all over us, but we should be kind, understanding, and earnestly pray for them. Romans 12:20 (AMPC) says, "But if your enemy is hungry, feed him; if he is thirsty, give him a drink; for by so doing you will heap burning coals upon his head." Upon first reading this, you might be thinking *yay, burning coals!* Why would you want to heap burning coals on someone's head? But that is not what the verse means. In Biblical times, people used coal to cook food and they carried these coals in a basket on their heads. Once we know this, the verse becomes clearer. You are helping the person! You might think being kind to someone who is harsh towards you is impossible. But when Christ lives in you, he works *through* you. Not in a magical, mystical way, but when we are in the Word daily and allow Him to change our minds, our tendency towards retaliation fades.

These principles are not easy to implement. It is a daily walk of choosing to do the right thing. Believe me, the Lord will give you plenty of opportunities to practice. As I used to say to the group home children I worked with, "Anybody can react and punch someone when attacked, but it takes a strong man or woman to pause, think it through, and do the right thing."

Sometimes, when we are not careful, we will guilt ourselves into co-dependency. What is co-dependency? It is when one person believes it's their job to save another by attending to every one of their needs. A co-dependent individual will build their whole identity around being a martyr, believing they must do everything for someone else because they cannot function without them. Co-dependency encourages learned helplessness, and the helper gets a sense of validation, which they have not achieved through healthier means.

I believe co-dependency is a big problem that often manifests in cases of elder abuse. Many people have elderly parents struggling to live independently, so they arrange to have Mom or Dad live with them, which is noble. I speak from experience; my mom lived with me for ten years until she passed at the age of 98.

The problems arise when the child starts resenting the parent for past hurts and doesn't discuss those hurts with them. While it's true the past can't be changed, it does not help to bury it. You might never know the reasons for your parent's behavior, and they may never ask for forgiveness, but it's essential to have honest conversations about your feelings. I know someone whose elderly mom could not fall asleep unless her daughter was home. Instead of developing healthy boundaries, the daughter would rush home so her mother could sleep. This behavior is not healthy. Healthy boundaries are needed so co-dependency doesn't grow.

When you step in every time there is a need, instead of letting the person figure out the problem independently, you are hurting them rather than helping them. I know people with a grown child or elderly parent living with them who never expect any help around the house, even when the person is quite capable. This can lead to anger and resentment in the caregiver and prevent the child or parent from participating in the joys and responsibilities of being part of a home.

Many organizations help those in need. As Christians, we also want to help; however, we must ask ourselves, "What if we feed the poor or donate to a great organization but never share Christ and fill spiritual needs?" People's earthly needs can be filled, but if they haven't accepted Christ as their Savior, they will still go to hell, except less hungry.

You perform a dual mission when you donate or participate in organizations that provide earthly help and share the Lord. Incorporating the Lord into the goal of helping others shows them that Jesus is a great God who wants to provide for them. We point people to Christ when they know our good deeds are because the Lord resides inside us. Bring Jesus into your conversations in a natural way. When I help my neighbor, I share where I stand with Jesus. I use the opportunity to talk about the Lord. In my work, I have never had a client say, "You have helped me with my problem, but don't tell me about your faith." They are always willing to hear what I say because I have shown concern and have willingly helped them.

I was in a store many years ago with my friend Nancy when the clerk accidentally gave her too much change. When Nancy pointed it out, the clerk was surprised and said, "Oh, thanks, that was really nice of you." Casually, Nancy replied, "That's fine. Jesus wouldn't want me to do anything else." Afterward, I told Nancy how impressed I was with how she gave Jesus credit for her actions.

"Treat people how you want to be treated" does not mean being silent and not addressing issues—quite the opposite. Jesus admonishes us in Matthew 18:15 (ESV), "If your brother sins against you, go and tell him his fault, between you and him alone. If he listens to you, you have gained your brother". It shows kindness to tell someone how they have hurt you, allowing them to correct the situation and explain themselves. This principle applies to all circumstances in life where you feel wronged.

Being faithful doesn't mean we expect Jesus to fix everything for us. God did not say, "Joshua, I want you to sit back while I deal with Jericho." Instead, God instructed Joshua to have his people walk around the city for seven consecutive days. On the seventh day, the trumpets were blown, and the people shouted. The walls tumbled to the ground. God did his part and instructed his people to do theirs! I encourage you to read Joshua 5:13–6:27, which details how God fought for His chosen people.

God doesn't want us to leave our common sense at the door but to use it. He equips us so we can. I often think about the Biblical story about an unsaved manager who was about to be fired. What did he do? The Bible says he didn't want to beg, so he approached individuals who owed his boss money and inquired how much they owed. Luke 16:6–8 (NLT) states, "The man replied, 'I owe him 800 gallons of olive oil.' So, the manager told him, 'Take the bill and quickly change it to 400 gallons.' 'And how much do you owe my employer?' he asked the next man. 'I owe him 1,000 bushels of wheat,' was the reply. 'Here,' the manager said, 'take the bill and change it to 800 bushels.' The rich man had to admire the dishonest rascal for being so shrewd. And it is true that the children of this world are shrewd in dealing with the world around them than are the children of the light."

The Lord isn't telling us to be dishonest but rather to understand the ways of the world and be "wise as serpents, and harmless as doves." (Matthew 10:16, KJV). We want the world to see the wisdom that God gives us when we follow His ways and pray before we act. As I've told my children, "Sometimes you have to speak up for those who won't speak up for themselves." When issues arise, we should see them as opportunities to stand up for ourselves and help others facing similar challenges.

I used to tell my co-workers in the emergency room, "If it weren't for the issues and problems that come our way, they could hire robots to work for a lot less." Facing our worries and troubles strengthens our mental health because we don't let complications fester and weigh on our minds. We can then deal with the issues and move forward.

"Treat people how you want to be treated" means honoring yourself and others. As we grow with the Lord, we learn to accept criticism without "getting our back up," and we learn to give positive, non-confrontational feedback. Practice using *The sandwich method:* **Say something good, Say what you need to say, and End with something positive.**

One of my favorite quotes is by Oliver Wendell Holmes: "Most people are willing to take the Sermon on the Mount as a flag to sail under, but few will use it as a rudder by which to steer." Biblical principles should not be just read; they should be lived. We must use the Word of God as a foundation for our lives. A past pastor of mine used to say, "Every time I think of doing something wrong, a thousand verses start running through my head." That's an excellent guide for staying on the right path.

2
LET GO

"For if you forgive other people when they sin against you, your heavenly Father will also forgive you. But if you do not forgive others their sins, your Father will not forgive your sins."

—Mathew 6:14-15 (NIV)

We know Matthew 6:14–15 is not talking about the forgiveness of sins for eternal salvation. Our salvation rests solely on Christ's finished work at the cross, not on our actions. Instead, it refers to Christ working through us and in us. It's about living a life that glorifies Christ so he will welcome us and say, "Well done, good and faithful servant!" (Matthew 25:21, NIV). It is knowing God is pleased with you and showing Himself strong on your behalf. What if God forgives your sins as you have forgiven others? That's certainly something to think about.

I've heard many people say, "I forgive him, but I don't want anything to do with him." Is this how God deals with us? There is a difference between reconciliation and forgiveness. However, as I tell my clients, "If you refuse to reconcile with the person who has hurt you, there should be two criteria:

1. The person is unrepentant and refuses to confess or admit their sin.
2. You are sure the person will do it again because you have forgiven them before.

The Bible tells us to forgive "70 times 7"—not as a literal 490 times, but as an example of forgiving freely and continuously. How can we truly practice this if, after the first time we forgive, we cut ties with the person? Without engaging with the person, the practice of forgiveness is incomplete.

Don't be a grudge holder or a "bean coun-ter," figuratively speaking. This mindset can destroy relationships. You might wonder why a friend stops talking to you, only to discover it was over something trivial that happened long ago, something you've completely forgotten. Meanwhile, they've been dwelling on it, allowing it to steal their joy and cloud their perspective on life.

It's different when you do things for someone because you *want* to, not because you *have* to. You'll find joy in bringing happiness to others. Unfortunately, this concept is lost on some who don't realize what they're missing. Over time, I've learned that when nothing is reciprocated, I start holding back. That's natural, we're only human. Plus, creating a bit of distance might be necessary with some people. It's better to establish healthy boundaries than to continue doing things resentfully.

My family is a family of givers. I like giving gifts to people I care about! But I had a friend who was quite the opposite. She hated Christmas shopping for things "people don't need." I explained to her that gift-giving isn't always about giving something that's needed. It's about showing someone they are cared for by putting thought into their gift. When Jesus said, "It is more blessed to give than to receive." (Acts 20:35, NKJV), that is what he meant. That is what the Christmas spirit is all about, except it should be all year long. We should always provide acts of service. Let people know you care; call them up to ask how they are doing. Be present.

You might have heard that adage in Sunday school—*Jesus, Others, Yourself* spells **JOY**. They were not kidding. Focusing on who you can encourage or how you can brighten someone's day is the key to thinking beyond yourself and bringing joy to your soul.

I must take a moment here to brag about my son, Scott. While in the Marines, he had a buddy whose grandmother in Poland was going through tough times. Without telling anyone, Scott got her address and began secretly sending her money. When the family found out, they were shocked and overwhelmed by his kindness. In gratitude, they invited him to spend Christmas with them in their home.

Afterward, when Scott came home, he said, "Can you believe they bought me a leather jacket?" I nodded because, while it is rare for an 18-year-old to send his hard-earned money to a stranger, for Scott, it was simply the right thing to do. He has a true gift for giving. What a wonderful spirit to have.

Is forgiveness always returned in kind? Absolutely not! It is all too *natural* to reject those who reject us. But instead of holding on to hurt, we should turn it over to the Lord. The keyword in that sentence is *natural.* Christ is calling on us to be *unnatural.* To be Christ-like means going against the flesh.

Galatians 5:17 (NKJV) states, "For the flesh lusts against the Spirit, and the Spirit against the flesh; and these are contrary to one another, so that you do not do the things that you wish." The word of God really does have an answer for everything! The struggle between flesh and spirit is why many Christians fall by the wayside; they don't want to give up anything for Christ. They view their acceptance of God as a one-time experience but don't want to commit to the Lord.

It is so easy to let the flesh guide our lives. We just do what we naturally want to do. We must be diligent to live our lives to reflect Christ by not being judgmental, loving those who despise us (Luke 6:27-28), and praying for those who have hurt us. That is the real struggle. I'm not pointing a finger at you— I'm pointing three back at me!

This doesn't mean you should be a people pleaser. Are you a people pleaser? People pleasers are often the person others consider sweet because of all they do. In fact, people pleasers can't say no and are frequently taken advantage of by those who recognize their inability to say no. If you think you might be a people-pleaser, consider this: Wouldn't it be better to say yes to the things you genuinely want to do and have more time for Bible reading, prayer, family, and friends? It seems Americans have bought into the idea that self-worth is tied to how many activities they are involved in. The busier they are, the more spiritual they are.

Billy Graham once said, "If I had to do my life over again, I would spend more time with the Lord." How powerful is that? These are the words of a man who taught, preached, and led thousands to Christ, yet, near the end of his life, he wished he had spent more time with Jesus.

Christians are often busy following God's calling, but is that what the Lord wants them to do? In Bible College, I heard, "Don't bother me now, Lord. I'm too busy doing your will." It's funny, or is it? We need to let go of the things that are not helping us move closer in our walk with the Lord, or at least cut back.

No one likes being mistreated, nor should we allow it. However, we should not be shocked when it happens. Jesus was treated terribly, although He was absolutely perfect. It doesn't get much worse than being crucified. And what did He say on the cross?

> "Father forgive them; for they know not what they do."

—Luke 23:34 (KJV)

3
SOW GOOD SEEDS

"And let us not grow weary while doing good, for in due season we shall reap if we do not lose heart. Therefore, as we have opportunity, let us do good to all, especially to those who are of the household of faith."

—Galatians 6:9–10 (NKJV)

I used to tell the group home children, "You are planting watermelon seeds and surprised when you are not getting tomatoes." It sounds silly, but that is what many people do. They spend their money foolishly, sometimes eating fast food four or five times a week, and wonder where their money goes. Or they continue to date the wrong type of person because they don't want to be lonely, not because the person is someone they truly enjoy.

Notice the verse says *in due season*. Just

because you do the right thing today doesn't mean all your problems will be solved by tomorrow. Isn't that exactly how it goes for dieters? They eat everything they are supposed to one day, then the next day, they're shocked to find out they didn't lose five pounds!

The phrase *reaping what you sow* is usually used with a bad connotation. It is rarely applied in a positive way. But, if you sow good seeds, you will reap good things. Remember this promise from II Chronicles 16:9 (NKJV), "For the eyes of the LORD run to and fro throughout the whole earth, to show Himself strong on behalf of *those* whose heart *is* loyal to Him." That's what I want in my life. I want the Lord to show me favor. But how can I ask the Lord to take care of my diabetes or heart issues if I fail to take care of my body? This doesn't mean we shouldn't ask for His help, but it does mean we should take responsibility for our part.

I used to believe in a *magical* God, asking Him to do things for me that He had already equipped me to do. I'm not saying God isn't in the miracle business because He most certainly is. But many times, He wants to empower us to take action. The road to change is not an easy road; it is a day-by-day, step-by-step process. That's one of the reasons AA is so successful. They never tell people that they can't take a drink for the rest of their lives. They emphasize making day-by-day, hour-by-hour decisions.

Examining the concept of the *magical* God can change your life. God empowers us to do what He has laid on our hearts. He doesn't do everything for us, but He gives His word as the foundation of our lives so we can make thoughtful and wise decisions. I wish I had known about this empowerment earlier in my life. I wanted to follow the Lord, but I was unprepared for the effort it would take. Still, I'm glad I instilled this in my children; if it was easy, it might not be worth it. Real accomplishment takes real effort. I love the verse, "If you have faith as small as a mustard seed, you can say to this mountain, 'Move from here to there, and it will move; nothing will be impossible for you'" (Matthew 17:20 NKJV)

If God tells you to do something through His word, He will provide you with the power and strength to do it. Prayer is our first resort; then get up and move in His direction. But remember, if it's worth doing, it probably won't be easy.

It takes determination to become the man or woman the Lord desires you to be. Will you fail? Of course. The key is to recognize your failures, learn from them, and ask God for forgiveness. If you hurt someone, go to them and make it right. As James 4:10 (KJV) says, "Humble yourselves in the sight of the Lord, and he shall lift you up." Support your children in their endeavors but allow them to fail—they will thank you for it later. I'm waiting—I'm waiting.

Joseph was the perfect example of a man determined to sow good seeds, regardless of the consequences. His commitment to doing what was right in God's eyes was evident throughout his life. Genesis 37–50 recounts the story of Joseph, the great-grandson of Abraham. Joseph's father, Jacob, had 12 sons who would become the 12 tribes of Israel. However, Joseph and Benjamin were the only sons born to Rachel, the wife Jacob truly loved. The other ten sons were born to Leah.

The ten brothers were jealous of Joseph because their father, Jacob, favored him. And when Jacob gave Joseph a coat of many colors, their jealousy further deepened. (You might remember the tale if you're familiar with the musical *Joseph and the*

Amazing Technicolor Dream Coat.) One day, Jacob asked Joseph to bring lunch to his ten brothers. When Joseph arrived, they decided to throw him into a pit. Soon after, some men from Egypt passed by, and the brothers chose to sell Joseph into slavery.

When Joseph arrived in Egypt, he was sold to Potiphar, one of Pharaoh's officials. Most people in this situation would be resentful and bitter, but not Joseph! His hard work, diligence, and integrity earned him Potiphar's trust, and Joseph was made responsible for the whole house. However, Potiphar's wife also took notice of him and tried to seduce him. Joseph refused, saying in one of my favorite verses, Genesis 39:9 (KJV), "How then can I do this great wickedness, and sin against God?" It would have been easy for him to think, "I've done nothing wrong. Why did God put me here? No one will know—I might as well enjoy myself." But Joseph remained faithful. And what was his reward? He was thrown into prison. It seems that sometimes, no good deed goes unpunished.

Did Joseph become resentful and angry at this point? No! He was such a good worker that he was put in charge of all the prisoners. The guards noticed he was an intelligent, hardworking young man.

Eventually, Pharaoh's chief butler and baker offend Pharoah and are imprisoned. While in prison, they both have dreams, and the Lord reveals the meaning of each dream to Joseph. Joseph then tells the butler that Pharoah will restore his position and asks him to remember him when released. He then interprets the baker's dream, warning him that he will be hanged in three days—which happens.

Two years pass and the butler has forgotten all about Joseph. But God never has. During this time, Joseph has learned the Egyptian language and has grown into a man of wisdom. When Pharaoh has a dream and seeks someone to interpret it, the butler remembers Joseph. Pharaoh immediately demands that Joseph be brought before him. In Genesis 41:15 (NIV), Pharaoh says to Joseph, "I had a dream, and no one can interpret it. But I have heard it said of you that when you hear a dream, you can interpret it." Joseph once more refers to the Lord. "'I cannot do it,' Joseph replies to Pharoah, 'but God will give Pharoah the answer he desires." (Genesis 41:16, NIV)

And guess what? God, as always, comes through and gives Joseph the interpretation. Joseph informs Pharoah that Egypt will have seven good years followed by seven years of famine. Then, he gave Pharaoh a plan to save Egypt. God not only presented the problem, but he also gave Joseph the solution. Pharoah is so impressed by the plan that he puts Joseph in charge of all of Egypt—second only to Pharaoh. How can people say the Bible is boring? This is fascinating stuff.

Despite Joseph's hardships of slavery and prison, he remains faithful to God, continues to honor Him, and works diligently. I am confident that if Joseph had allowed his circumstances to determine his attitude, God would have found someone else to save Egypt. Set your mind to do your best for God even when in a place you don't want to be. Remember, God never forgets you. He always knows where you are and where to find you.

When you're not asked out, be faithful anyway. When you don't get the job, be faithful anyway. God might be closing doors on what you desire to open an amazing door that He wants for you. You just need to be *faithful!*

4
SURROUND YOURSELF WITH POSITIVE PEOPLE AND EXPERIENCES

Nothing can keep you from living your best life like people who are not living theirs. I used to tell my kids, "If you are standing on a chair, it is a lot easier for me to pull you down than for you to pull me up." I am a living, breathing miracle of God. I grew up in a very negative, depressed household, and I missed out on many activities in school because I didn't have anyone to encourage or support me, even when I wanted to participate. I didn't connect the Word of God to my daily life. I didn't recognize the amazing promises I had as a child of the King. In other words, I was a princess, and I didn't even know it.

When I discuss this concept with my clients, they roll their eyes and say, "I don't feel like a princess or prince." That's the great thing about being a child of God. It doesn't depend on how you feel; it's a fact.

I'm sure kings and queens living today and from long ago didn't always feel like "kinging."

> "For you are all sons of God
> through faith in Christ Jesus."
>
> —Galatians 3:26 (NKJV)

I have heard people say, "We are all children of God." That is not true. We are all creations of God, but we are not all His children, just like I am not a member of your family, no matter how close we become. I must be *born* into your family. The only way we can be *born* is to accept Christ's payment for our sins at the cross. Jesus made this very clear in John 14:6 (NKJV), saying, "I am the way, the truth, and the life. No one comes to the Father except through Me." You don't clean up your life and then come to Christ. You accept Him as Savior and let the Holy Spirit come into your life to give you the power and guidance to clean up the mess.

Surround yourself with positive people. Talk about experiences, not people. Facebook, Twitter, Instagram, and YouTube have turned us into extremely narcissistic individuals. I always say, "Show me your friends, and I'll show you your future." When

I worked in a group home, many kids hung around people who didn't care about them and weren't concerned about their future. But if your friends are doing well, going to college, and living a productive life, chances are you will too.

One of the principles of thriving in your Christian life is to have friends who are not only believers but are also excited about the Lord and want to live their lives for Jesus. Join a church that teaches the Word of God, a small group, or a Sunday school that will help you learn His word and provide fellowship with other believers. This was the case in my life. As of this writing, I learned my first pastor from Charlotte, Dr. Rick Blackwood, has passed away. I am heartbroken. Bible college taught me the Bible, but Rick taught me to love the Bible. He was a book-by-book, verse-by-verse teacher. We all grew in the Word with his expository preaching and grieved when he moved to Miami.

Aiming for thirty minutes a day of reading your Bible verse-by-verse and chapter-by-chapter is so important. You will never remember a teaching from someone else the same way you will when you discover it on your own. Just remember the Bible talks about various subjects in different places. You should look at the subject you are studying and find other places that discuss the same topic to get a comprehensive viewpoint. Today, this is so easy to accomplish through the internet. I recommend using *Bible Hub*. It lets you look up a passage in the Old Testament and find the Hebrew translation, the original language of the old covenant. And, when reading the New Testament, you can look up the passages in the Greek translation, the original text of the new covenant.

"No one is an island" is a famous saying that applies to Christian life. Many people come to know the Lord but have countless friends who do not know Him. It's a great witnessing opportunity! However, developing friendships with those further down the road in their Christian experience will help you grow in your faith. Taking time out of your busy schedule and creating relationships with others is time-consuming, but the benefits strengthen you.

Everyone is at a different point in their Christian walk. Some are weak, whereas some are strong, and vice versa. Just because I have been a Christian longer than you does not mean I can't learn from you. You might be stronger in an area where I struggle. We can all learn from each other in the body of Christ. A pastor I once knew said, "When the battery in your car goes dead, you don't get out and walk away." But that is *exactly* what we do in Christian life. If someone upsets us or does something we know isn't right, instead of working on the relationship, we walk away. Our friendships should be precious. Try talking with the person so you can both benefit.

Ask the Lord to send you someone to confide in and share your joys and sorrows. A true friend will stand by you in the hard times and rejoice over your successes. Proverbs 18:24 (KJV) reads, "A man that hath friends must shew himself friendly: and there is a friend that sticketh closer than a brother." But you will need to open yourself up and be able to forgive when the time comes because it will surely come. Being around different types of people helps you gain more experience and, if they are honest with you, can help you smooth the rough edges of your personality.

It is essential to develop a friendship with someone before you start dating. Too many young people today have a sexual relationship before they really know the person. God is not a joy killer. He is an amazing joy giver. That is why He wants us to wait for sex until we are married. He wants us to get to know the person as a friend in all types of situations, joys, sorrows, disappointments, and challenges, before we get to know them sexually. Marry your best friend; when hard times come, you will know what to expect and will be prepared to support your spouse.

5
TAKING CARE OF MY MIND AND BODY

First and foremost, *every* addiction begins in the mind. When people say, "I wasn't thinking I just did it." That is simply not true. Your mind always takes the first step in a meaningful way and can sometimes lead you down a slippery slope. It is not a food problem, it is a mind problem, it's not a drug problem, it's a mind problem. You can overcome anything if you get your mind on a firm foundation. But it takes a lot of work and determination.

> "But I keep under my body, and bring it into subjection: lest that by any means, when I have preached to others, I myself should be a castaway."
>
> —I Corinthians 9:27 (KJV)

In other words, if we don't take care of

ourselves, we might not be used the way God wants to use us. Think about this. Noah was 500 years old when God asked him to build the ark. If you keep in shape, you never know what God might ask you to do when you're 500 years old! Seriously, I plan to stay as healthy as I can in mind and body and then die fast. Hopefully, I'll be raptured.

> "For the Lord himself shall descend from heaven with a shout, with the voice of the archangel, and with the trump of God: and the dead in Christ shall rise first."
>
> —I Thessalonians 4:16 (KJV)

The Bible says that God gave us plants and herbs for healing. Genesis 1:29 (ESV) says, "And God said, 'Behold, I have given you every plant yielding seed that is on the face of all the earth, and every tree with seed in its fruit. You shall have them for food.'" Do you know that man did not eat meat until after the flood? That is approximately 1656 years. In Genesis 9:3–4 (NIV), God tells us, "Everything that lives and moves about will be food for you. Just as I gave you the green plants, I now give you everything. But you must not eat meat that has its lifeblood still in it."

It is important to read the whole Word of God. The Bible does not have everything that pertains to a specific subject in one place. There are several passages all over the Bible pertaining to specific subjects. For example, Noah was instructed to take seven pairs of clean animals (not seven, seven *pairs*), male and female, and one pair of unclean animals; therefore, we understand by the passage in Genesis 9 that God means for them to eat of the clean and not the unclean animals. Why were they called unclean? Because God said so. It's easy to understand why shellfish because they are bottom feeders, but boy, am I glad we are not under the law when it comes to lobster and crab legs. However, why deer, rabbit, bear, alligator, and all the other types of animals? This is where faith comes in. God blesses us for obedience even when we don't understand. There are passages where God tells us what to eat and what not to eat all over the scriptures. But because we are in the time of grace, not the law, we should look at how God tells us to take care of our bodies.

In Acts 10:10–16 (NIV), we read about Peter having a dream called the great white sheet. Peter goes up to the roof to pray. Don't miss this! Peter was talking to the Lord about wanting to live by His Word. "'He became hungry and wanted something to eat, and while the meal was being prepared, he fell into a trance. He saw heaven opened and something like a large sheet being let down to earth by its four corners. It contained all kinds of four-footed animals, as well as reptiles and birds. Then a voice told him, 'Get up, Peter. Kill and eat.' 'Surely not, Lord!' Peter replied. 'I have never eaten anything impure or unclean' The voice spoke to him a second time, 'Do not call anything impure that God has made clean.'This happened three times, and immediately the sheet was taken back to heaven.'"

A lot of people familiar with this passage will say the vision was given to Peter so he would know the gospel was open to the Gentiles. In other words, it is open to everyone, not just the Jews, to partake of salvation. That is definitely true. However, God never uses a false illustration to show us the truth. The vision has a double meaning. All food is acceptable since Christ came to fulfill the law; we are not under the law, but grace, and the gospel belongs to everyone. This principle can be seen in communion. It is not the elements representing the blood and body of Christ themselves but is a *remembrance* of His death on the cross and His eternal payment for our sins.

Now that we are under grace, should we eat and drink anything we desire? No as I said before, we are to take care of ourselves and be in subjection to Christ in this area. In Matthew 6:25 (KJV), Jesus says, "Therefore I say unto you, Take no thought for your life, what ye shall eat, or what ye shall drink; nor yet for your body, what ye shall put on. Is not the life more than meat, and the body than raiment?" Does this mean it is wrong to think about what you are having for dinner tonight or what you wear to church? No, of course not. It means we should not be *overly* obsessed with food or our appearance. Obesity and anorexia are in the same category. It is the thinking about food constantly that is the problem.

I know this from experience. There was a period of time in my teens when I became anorexic. At the time, people didn't understand its psychological roots and weren't talking about the disease. As I started reading the Bible in college, I realized that thinking about food had a lot of power over me. So, I memorized the verses that addressed my problem. "I can do all things through him who strengthens me." (Philippians 4:13, ESV). "Take no thought for your life, what you shall eat, or what ye shall drink." (Matthew 6:25 KJV). These verses became a mantra to me. I would repeat them and ask God for deliverance from food's control over me.

Overeating, like all sin, starts in the mind. Satan wants you to think about anything except Jesus Christ and what He wants to do in your life. I started investigating nutrition and concentrating on nourishing my body, not just feeding it. I was in a battle. And like all battles, there are some wins and some losses. As I became more involved with reading God's word, prayer, fellowshipping with others, and witnessing, food lost its grip on me. I was no longer a slave to thinking about food. It no longer had power over me. I believe many people fail at breaking addictions because they are concentrating on their addiction instead of focusing on the scriptures and the power of God's Word to change their lives.

Many diets fail because people think if they eat or don't eat a particular food they will lose weight. We all know people who have had gastric bypass and other surgeries to lose weight. They lose it and then gain it all back. Why is this? The biggest reason is that they forget they have a heavenly Father who is showing Himself strong on their behalf and that the Holy Spirit is there to help them with their weaknesses. We are working on the *FRUIT* of the problem, not the *ROOT* of the problem. Working on the *ROOT* makes all the difference. I'm not saying it is an easy road, but as in *AA*, when you have a mentor, you have the Holy Spirit living and breathing inside of you.

Realizing you have the power of the Holy Spirit within you does not mean you can pray, and that is the end of it. It doesn't mean you sit on the couch and let the Lord do the work! Quite the contrary, it is just the beginning of the road ahead of you. You next have to start down the path of taking care of yourself the way God designed you to. We live in a fallen world, which is why we should keep our minds focused on Christ. I tell my clients to write down five verses related to their situation. I instruct them to put them on index cards and keep the verses with them until they're embedded in their minds.

Imagine you have a problem controlling your weight. You go to your friend's house, and they have all your favorite foods. We are meant to be in community. God designed us to fellowship with other believers and to reach out to the unsaved; that being said, refusing invitations because *I am on a diet* is not the way to handle this temptation. Instead, I use my five memorized verses.

Let's see how this works:

> "I can do all things through Christ who strengthens me."
>
> —Philippians 4:13 (NKJV)
>
> How do I put this into prac-tice? Lord, you know I am being tempted. Help me not to give in to the temptation of putting too much food on my plate.

"There hath no temptation taken you, but such as is common to man: but God is faithful, who will not suffer you to be tempted above that ye are able; but will with the temptation also make a way to escape, that ye may be able to bear it." (I Corinthians 10:13, KJV). This verse reminds me that I am facing something many others have faced. But how do I thwart this temptation? First, I don't go to dinner starving! I eat a couple of crackers with cheese before going. It is surprising how little it takes to make you feel satisfied when you listen to your body. A lot of Americans don't know anything about really feeling hungry.

> "Take no thought for your life,
> what ye shall eat…"
>
> —Matthew 6:25 (KJV)
>
> Don't dwell on food; focus on the
> friends and the company providing
> the food.

"When you sit to dine with a ruler, note well what is before you, and put a knife to your throat if you are given to gluttony. Do not crave his delicacies, for that food is deceptive." (Proverbs 23:1–3, NIV). This does not mean you put a knife to your throat. That would probably take your name off the next dinner party guest list. Instead, it is saying to control yourself. Often, we eat like it is our last meal. Take smaller portions!

> "But put on the Lord Jesus Christ
> and make no provision for the flesh
> in regard to its lusts."
>
> —Romans 13:14. (NASB)

> Make no provision. Determine ahead of time. I will not come to dinner starving. I am not going to keep eating until I feel stuffed. I'm going to eat more salads, vegetables, and smaller amounts of carbs.

The more you practice mindful eating, the easier it will become. This same principle works for all addictions. We often hear pastors talk about drugs, porn, smoking, and alcohol addictions, but very rarely hear them talk about over-eating as a sin. Why is this? Look around at the Christian community, and you will see the answer. It is simply not looked upon as a sin. Why? Because many Christians are doing it! The Bible talks about fasting a lot, yet we rarely hear that being talked about either.

Food and weight control are a form of fasting when you deny yourself because you want to take care of your body as a temple of Christ. I Corinthians 6:19-20 (ESV) says, "Or do you not know that your body is a temple of the Holy Spirit within you, whom you have from God? You are not your own, for you were bought with a price. So, glorify God in your body." What was that price? God sent Jesus Christ to die for you. If you go to hell, it is literally over Christ's body since He already paid the sin payment for you.

When I worked in the emergency room, I was known as the pizza lady because I would draw a circle and split it in half. One side represents your job, and the other your family.

Circle 1:

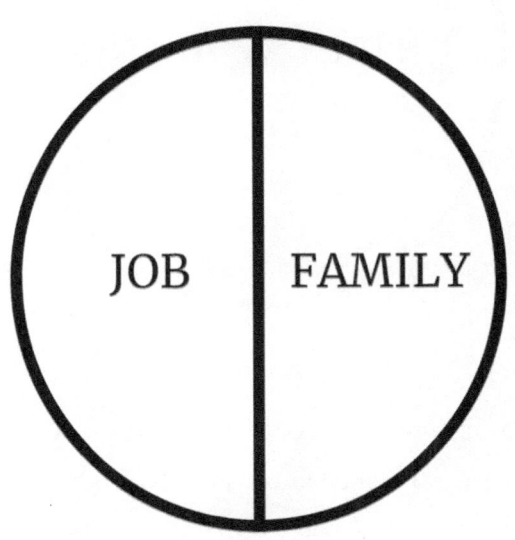

Next, I'd draw another circle with six slices. Each slice listed one item: job, family, friends, hobbies, community, and faith-based activities (such as

TAG-time alone with God in His word, praying, or fellowship with other Christians.)

Circle 2:

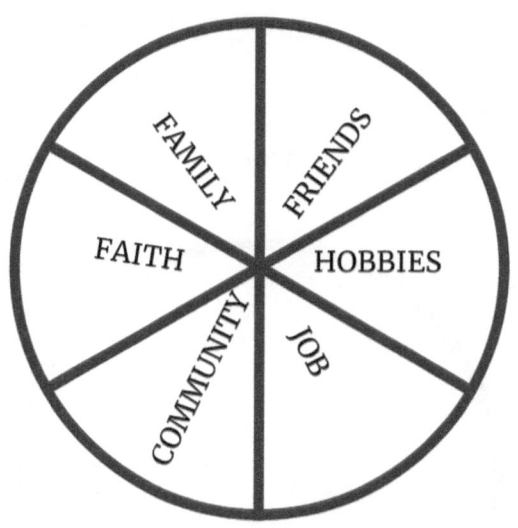

    Suppose you go to work one day and discover your job has been outsourced, and you are out of work! In *Circle 1* you can see that amounts to 50% of your life. Where you once had a job, it has been replaced by fear, anxiety, anger, regret, and other negative emotions.

    Next, take the same scenario and apply it to

Circle 2. However, in the second scenario, the job only incorporated 1/6 or 16.6% of your life. That is quite a difference! There are so many things in life we cannot control. We can lose a family member, our health, or our job. Even when we believe we have control over our lives, life can spin around on a dime.

This illustration hits home for a lot of people. Everybody can remember a pizza and understand the importance of having several interests in life. John 10:10 (KJV) says, "I am come that they might have life, and that they might have it more abundantly." Christians should be the happiest people on earth. Not that we won't have problems, for Jesus tells us that in this life, we will have troubles, John 16:33. But He promises that He will be with us through them.

As a Christian, you can use these figures to help you overcome any addiction. Having the Holy Spirit in your life gives you the power to be an overcomer. "For whatever is born of God overcomes the world. And this is the victory that has overcome the world—our faith." (I John 5:4, NKJV). You can call on Him because you have the promise that He hears you.

"Now this is the confidence that we have in Him, that if we ask anything according to His will, He hears us."

—I John 5:14, NKJV)

A recipe to help with any addiction:

- First, recognize your sin and ask the Lord to come into your life and save you.
- Second, ask God for deliverance and start having TAG—time alone with God every day, in His Word and in prayer.
- Third, look at the pizza circle. How many slices do you have in your life's pie? What can you put into your life? Addiction of any kind takes a lot of time, money, and secret behaviors. Come "… out of the darkness into His marvelous light." (I Peter 2:9, NASB). Think about the pieces in your life's pie and concentrate on them. Consider

taking up a new hobby, learning something new, or spending more quality time with family.

In psychology, there's a study where you tell a group of people they cannot think about the color yellow while you are talking. What do you think happens? Right! At the end of the study group, the teacher asks, "What did I tell you not to think about?" Everybody responds, "The color yellow!" It's funny, but a lot of mental health workers approach addiction the same way. They encourage the person to think about the addiction constantly instead of thinking about other things they could be doing. As a Christian, you have the power of the Holy Spirit within you; He will help you and give you strength. It will be a hard road, but when you have the Holy Spirit inside of you, He can provide you with the strength to stop drinking, smoking, taking drugs, watching pornography, engaging in sex outside of marriage, over-eating, or any other addiction.

When my clients tell me they are going to beat their addiction, I tell them, "Great. What are you going to start doing instead?" Most of the time, they stare at me as if they haven't given it any thought. Your addiction controls a lot of your life. If you think you are going to stop and not replace it with something else that fills the time and satisfaction you received from the addiction, you are kidding yourself. So find something enjoyable to help fill the emptiness. This is why Christian fellowship is so important. I don't mean just going to church. I mean having a group of people that will encourage you in your faith.

This principle can be helped with what I call *The Power of the Temporal.* What do I mean? Well, Americans, by in large, are goal-driven. We strive not to give up and be the best we can be, which is good, except when you consider most of us will never be Olympians. This is why I refer to it as the power of the temporal.

I wrote an article about this topic, so let me explain further. Sometimes, we hesitate to start learning a musical instrument because we know we won't make it into the orchestra, or we avoid running because we don't want to run a marathon. We might even skip taking a French class because we're not planning a trip to France, so why bother, but who cares if you just use it for yourself or only for six months? The fear of not achieving great success often keeps us from trying. I believe this is why many retirees struggle to enjoy their retirement. After working hard their entire lives, they spend their days watching TV or engaging in activities that don't give them a sense of accomplishment.

Mental health workers need to encourage people to branch out. There are so many wonderful things to learn, experience, and enjoy. The world is a big place, and there are a lot of exciting experiences to enjoy. About three years ago, I took up the violin. I practiced every day and was sure I was going to make the church orchestra. However, my clients and writing kept calling me to my first love. Am I sorry I took up the violin? No way! Will you see me in the orchestra someday? No way!

How do you keep inertia from setting in? Remember what I said, "The world is a big place, and it's okay if you fail." Most of us reflect on our lives and regret the things we didn't do. Such as: not dating someone because we don't want to marry them, not taking a job because we're not sure we want to be there for 20 years, not moving because we might not like the new place, or not going on a short-term mission because we've never been away from home. But, if you have the Lord, He is going to go there with you. You can't leave him behind. The Holy Spirit lives within you.

No one can honestly say, "I didn't think about it; I just did it." Our mind guides how we will act, think, and conduct ourselves. I Corinthians 2:16–17 (KJV) says, "For who hath known the mind of the Lord, that he may instruct him? but we have the mind of Christ." In other words, as believers, we have the mind of Christ, if we are in the Word, so the Lord can teach us, not the other way around.

It is important to be careful about the things you watch, the people you associate with, and the activities in which you get involved. It is too easy to be negatively influenced in this world. There are plenty of distractions. Psalm 101:3 (NKJV) says, "I will set nothing wicked before my eyes; I hate the work of those who fall away; it shall not cling to me." Everything around us can easily distract us. I like what Davis says in Psalms 132:3–5 (NASB). "I certainly will not enter my house, nor lie on my bed; I will not give sleep to my eyes or slumber to my eyelids, Until I find a place for the LORD, A dwelling place for the Mighty One of Jacob."

How do you develop a love and a desire for God's word? Pray! I know people who go from Bible study to Bible study but admit that their prayer life is almost nonexistent. When you search the scriptures, you see how often Jesus left the people to go pray. If Jesus felt the need to talk to His Father, how can we do anything less? Pray and ask the Lord to help you understand His Word. Did you know that one of the Holy Spirit's jobs is to teach us the Scriptures? John 14:26 (KJV) reads, "But the Comforter, which is the Holy Ghost, whom the Father will send in my name, he shall teach you all things, and bring all things to your remembrance, whatsoever I have said unto you." The only problem is the keyword ***REMEMBRANCE***. We can't remember what we have never learned. Most of the verses I have quoted are from memory, but I don't necessarily recall where the verse is located. Thank you, Google.

Suppose you have an anxiety issue. Look up and put five verses about anxiety on index cards and carry them with you. When you feel anxious, think about the verses; you will be surprised at how the Holy Spirit will bring them to your mind and give you strength amid a crisis.

Devotionals and Christian books are excellent resources, but they are not a substitute for God's Word on your heart. People talk about being busy, but they can go on and on about a TV program or a hobby they enjoy. There is nothing wrong with these things, but you must make time for God, or you will never get to know Him. It is a daily step-by-step walk.

It takes approximately six weeks to develop a new habit. So, set up a strategy. Try reading your Bible first thing in the morning. Get up half an hour earlier to have quiet time between you and the Lord. You will find your life transformed by the renewing of your mind. "Therefore, I urge you, brothers and sisters, in view of God's mercy, to offer your bodies as a living sacrifice, holy and pleasing to God —this is your true and proper worship. Do not conform to the pattern of this world but be transformed by the renewing of your mind. Then you will be able to test and approve what God's will is—his good, pleasing and perfect will" (Romans 12:1–2, NIV). What great news!

Many people have grown up with fearful, grudging, depressed, anxiety-filled, unforgiving, narcissistic, revenge-seeking parents, to name a few. Isn't it wonderful that, even if you were surrounded by wrong thinking during your formative years, God specializes in cleansing, renewing, and transforming our minds? In my walk with Christ, I am always amazed that Jesus can change my mind about things I didn't know needed changing. By committing my mind to Christ, I become more like Him.

Renewing your mind is a *daily* process. Psalm 1:1–2 (NKJV) says, "Blessed *is* the man Who walks not in the counsel of the ungodly, Nor stands in the path of sinners, Nor sits in the seat of the scornful; But his delight *is* in the law of the LORD, And in His law he meditates day and night."

Once you start reading the Word and stick with it, you will learn to love it. It is a lot like committed runners. They don't wake up and say, "I think I'll run a marathon today.". No, they start by running for maybe half an hour per day. They don't love it every day, but they keep at it, working toward a goal—fitness and achievement. They have good days and bad days, but the bad does not deter them. They are running towards a goal, only it's short-lived, not eternal.

How much time should we commit to an eternal goal? How much to a goal that will renew our minds, give us joy in this life, and an everlasting value? I Corinthians 9:24–27 (NIV) tells us, "Do you not know that in a race all the runners run, but only one gets the prize? Run in such a way as to get the prize. Everyone who competes in the games goes into strict training. They do it to get a crown that will not last, but we do it to get a crown that will last forever. Therefore, I do not run like someone running aimlessly; I do not fight like a boxer beating the air. No, I strike a blow to my body and make it my slave so that after I have preached to others, I will not be disqualified from the prize." (Psalm 119:11). Wow! We not only have eternal prizes but have so much to gain in this life by hiding God's word in our hearts.

Commit to prayer! I know a lot of people who go to Bible studies, watch Christian movies, read devotionals, and know the Bible but admit prayer is not a big part of their lives. I remember a song I used to sing repeatedly when I was around five. It goes like this.

> When I forget to say my prayers,
> the devil shouts with glee, but he
> feels so awful, awful when he sees
> me on my knees. So, if you're full of

trouble and you never seem to win
just open up your heart and let the
sunshine in. So let the sunshine in
face it with a grin. Smilers never
lose, and frowners never win, so
let the sunshine in, face it with a
grin, open up your heart, and let
the sunshine in.

—Stuart Hamblen, And Let The
Sun Shine In

When the Bible tells us to pray without ceasing, as in I Thessalonians 5:17, it is telling us we should always be in an attitude of prayer and seeking closeness to God. How do you do that? The same way you develop a friendship. You spend time, share your thoughts and ideas, show an interest, and get to know Him.

I've had clients who say they are close to the Lord, but they do not read their Bible. This is impossible. The Bible is God's love letter to us. It is the only way we can know about the Father, Son, and Holy Spirit. The movie *A Walk In The Clouds* tells the story of the main character, portrayed by Keanu Reeves, who goes off to war. He and his wife are married for a very short time before he leaves. So, he writes to his wife almost every day. When he returns, he's surprised when she does not meet him, so he asks her why. She replies that she didn't know he was coming home. "But I wrote you almost every day," he says. In response, his wife pulls out a trunk full of unopened letters. "I couldn't read them. I was too scared," She explains. Disappointed, he realizes his wife really didn't know much about him.

I believe this is the main reason that, like the world, Christians are falling apart. They are afraid, anxious, depressed, guarded, and unforgiving. If you don't know God's Word, you will act like the world when life throws you a huge curve. When we are in the Word and have close communication with God through the Word, He calms our souls in the midst of the storm. "The Word became flesh and made his dwelling among us. We have seen his glory, the glory of the one and only Son, who came from the Father, full of grace and truth." I love the song lyric from *Sometimes He Calms The Storm* by Scott Krippayne. It says: "Sometimes He calms the storm, but most of the time He calms His child." Let Jesus calm your soul in the midst of the storm.

6

FORGIVENESS, RESTORATION, SEPARATION AND DIVORCE

Forgiveness, restoration, separation, and divorce are hot topics full of condemnation in the Christian church these days. This is because some verses are misinterpreted. But, when you examine the whole Word of God, it's easy to understand them. You don't have to go to seminary, but you should study the Bible daily. Try to memorize some scripture as you study verse-by-verse and book-by-book. It's well worth the time and effort.

Forgiveness and restoration are two very different things. You can forgive someone who doesn't ask for forgiveness, is dead, doesn't understand why the issue is a *big deal,* or does not acknowledge your hurt and their sin. Restoration, on the other hand, involves both parties. There has to be repentance, an acknowledgment of sin, a desire to *make it right,* and confidence in the other parties' commitment to real change.

I have heard many Christians say, "I forgive them, but I don't want anything to do with them." This is unscriptural. People get hurt but refuse to confront the person responsible. When I moved from New Jersey to North Carolina, I was astounded to see the amount of people who shut down and refused to speak with the person who hurt them. They seem to believe it is better to ignore the issue rather than, as God commands, speak directly to the person.

Every believer should be familiar with this passage. It is a friend-saver! Read it carefully; there's a lot to unpack!

> "If your brother sins against you, go and tell him his fault, between you and him alone. If he listens to you, you have gained your brother. But if he does not listen, take one or two others along with you, that every charge may be established by the evidence of two or three witnesses. If he refuses to listen to them, tell it to the church. And if he refuses to listen even to the church, let him be to you as a Gentile and a

tax collector."

—Matthew 18:15–17, (ESV).
Wow! There's a lot here.

Let's dissect this: First, go to him *alone*. When I first started working in the emergency room, I was a liaison between the patients and staff. My job was to work out the issues between the two. As a bona fide Yankee, I loved dealing with all the problems that arose. At first, the staff were uneasy when I addressed an issue. So, I talked to them alone and reassured them our conversations were confidential. I didn't understand their fear. When I asked someone about this, I found out the problem. A lot of people went to a supervisor without first approaching the individual. They were trying to keep people from retaliating, which can happen, but it further created distrust between co-workers. As the staff got to know me, they began to appreciate my use of humor and what I call the sandwich technique: *Say something good, Say what you need to say, and End with something positive.*

After the first year, at my performance review, my boss said, "I couldn't find anybody that said anything bad about you." I was astounded, especially since I had addressed multiple issues. However, I had treated everyone with respect. I'd apologized when they felt I'd been remiss in immediately handling a situation, and I had a sincere desire for them to feel heard and respected.

Have you ever had a problem with a friend and, after resolving it, felt closer to them? This is the goal, not to have a friendship where you are *walking on eggshells* and need to watch what you say, but to have a bond where you can talk about situations that come up and appreciate your friend for being honest with you. I love Proverbs 27:6 (KJV), "Faithful are the wounds of a friend; but the kisses of an enemy are deceitful."

The next part of the verse discusses bringing two or three witnesses for more severe offenses, where other people's involvement is needed, or when there is a refusal to acknowledge the offense and repent. Having witnesses can provide a better perspective of the situation as a third party sees it. Finally, if the offender's heart is still hard, we are to go to the church, not to the whole congregation, but to the governing body, i.e., the deacons, pastor, and possibly the elders.

If the offender refuses to listen, he should be

as a tax collector or gentile. These people were not allowed in the synagogue because even though the tax collectors were Jewish, they were participating in the robbery of their fellow Jews. The Romans would demand a percentage of the Jewish peoples' income, let's say 25% for this example. But, the tax collector could charge whatever he felt like, as long as the Romans received their 25%. It's easy to see why there was so much animosity toward the tax collectors. They were hated! When Jesus called Matthew, the tax collector, to be a disciple, it was shocking to the Pharisees. Matthew 9:11 (NIV) talks about the calling of Matthew. When the Pharisees saw Jesus eating with his disciples, they asked his disciples, "Why does your teacher eat with tax collectors and sinners?" In their opinion, eating with the tax collectors was the same as eating with the Gentiles, which was forbidden by Jewish law.

In Matthew 18:15–17, the person who refuses to repent of their sin should be made to leave the church. It is the same principle that Paul faced when he visited the church in Corinth. I Corinthians 5:1–13 is a perfect passage to glean how church discipline should be handled today.

"It is actually reported that there is fornication among you, and such fornication as is not even among the Gentiles, that one *of you* hath his father's wife. And ye are puffed up, and did not rather mourn, that he that had done this deed might be taken away from among you. For I verily, being absent in body but present in spirit, have already as though I were present judged him that hath so wrought this thing, in the name of our Lord Jesus, ye being gathered together, and my spirit, with the power of our Lord Jesus, to deliver such a one unto Satan for the destruction of the flesh, that the spirit may be saved in the day of the Lord Jesus. Your glorying is not good. Know ye not that a little leaven leaveneth the whole lump? Purge out the old leaven, that ye may be a new lump, even as ye are unleavened. For our Passover also hath been sacrificed, *even* Christ. Wherefore let us keep the feast, not with old leaven, neither with the leaven of malice and wickedness, but with the unleavened bread of sincerity and truth. I wrote unto you in my epistle to have no company with fornicators; not at all *meaning* with the fornicators of this world, or with the covetous and extortioners, or with idolaters; for then must ye needs go out of the world: but as it is, I wrote unto you not to keep company, if any man that is named a brother be a fornicator, or covetous, or an idolater, or a reviler, or a drunkard, or an extortioner; with such a one no, not to eat. For what have I to do with judging them that are without? Do not ye judge them that are within? But them that are without God judgeth. Put away the wicked man from among yourselves."

—I Corinthians 5:1–13 (ASV)

In this passage, *within* refers to those who are saved, meaning those who are part of the church—not a specific church building, but the body of Christ as a whole. *Without* pertains to those who are outside the family of God, those who are not believers.

I know this is a lot, but both passages refer to the same thing. Christians should be asked to leave the church if they refuse to repent and be restored through genuine repentance of their sin. However, when they repent, the church should reconcile with them. Excommunication was never created to toss someone out and refuse to allow them back. It was meant to soften the hardened heart so the person would want to recognize their sin and get back into fellowship.

How many churches have a program to restore a fallen believer? Very few! More often, the person leaves and joins another church, but what if the fallen believer is willing to go and talk about the circumstances of their sin with the church? I like how I Timothy 5:20 (NASB) puts it, "Those who continue in sin, rebuke in the presence of all, so that the rest also will be fearful of *sinning*." Did you catch the phrase, continue in sin? Excommunication is for those who refuse to repent. They should be asked to leave the church as a consequence of their repeated sin. By doing so, the hope is that they will come to repentance and be restored into the fellowship.

I was once in church when a man stood up and confessed his unfaithfulness to his wife. He talked about flirting at work. You could feel the discomfort. It was powerful. How many people are involved in pornography or other secret sins that would benefit from being confronted?

I once knew a believer who failed miserably and wanted to go in front of the church to ask forgiveness of the body of believers as the whole church was affected by his sin. He was refused twice by his pastor. Yet we wonder why we have so many failings and brokenness within the church. Sin is not being confronted, people are not hearing from the repentant, and those who have left the church are not being loved and mentored so they may seek repentance and return. What a testimony that would be to the fellowship of believers, to see those who have sinned being loved back into fellowship! Now, that would be a living example of true forgiveness.

As Christians we are missing a great opportunity. We hear about people who are forced to leave the church, but then no one knows or cares what happens to them. We are, for the most part, shooting our own wounded. I wish we had a formal restoration program where the church confronted people with known sins. This would decrease the number of sinners who fall away from God. Hearing someone confess to a sin that has been weighing on their mind and witnessing the consequences might give the witness second thoughts and encourage them to walk away from indulging behaviors. It is easy to see that Jesus knew confession would thwart some believers and that they would call on God for deliverance.

Why is it so hard for Christians to restore a fellow believer who has committed a grievous sin? The number one reason is unbelief. We sing songs all the time about how all sins are left at the cross. Jesus forgives all, but do we incorporate those principles into our own lives? Think of the song *Redeemed* by Big Daddy Weave:

Seems like all I could see was the struggle
Haunted by ghosts that lived in my past
Bound up in shackles of all my failures
Wondering how long is this gonna last
Then you look at this prisoner and say to me

"Son, stop fighting a fight, it's already been won"

Chorus:

I am redeemed, You set me free
So, I'll shake off these heavy chains
Wipe away every stain
That I'm not who I used to be
I am redeemed, I'm redeemed

Verse 2:

All my life, I have been called unworthy
Named by the voice of my shame and regret
But when I hear you whisper, "Child,
lift up your head"
I remember, oh God, You're not done with me yet

Chorus:

I am redeemed, You set me free
So I'll shake off these heavy chains
Wipe away every stain
Now, I'm not who I used to be

Bridge:

Because I don't have to be the old man inside of me
'cause his day is long dead and gone
Because I've got a new name
A new life, I'm not the same

And a hope that will carry me home

Chorus 2:

I am redeemed, You set me free
So I'll shake off these heavy chains
And wipe away every stain
Cause I'm not who I used to be
I am redeemed, You set me free
So I'll shake off these heavy chains
And wipe away every stain
That I'm not who I used to be
Oh God, I'm not who I used to be
Jesus, I'm not who I used to be
Cause I am redeemed
Thank God redeemed

I love this song: it says it all. We are redeemed! Yet, we justify not having fellowship with those who have fallen into deep sin. We often don't call them to comfort them, and we react the same way the world does. We say and think things like, *They will do it again, they are not repentant, I don't trust them, I don't care what their story entails, or I would never do that.* The list goes on and on.

We forget that we are commanded to have

the ministry of reconciliation. 2 Corinthians 5:18–21 (NIV) talks about this ministry. "All this is from God, who reconciled us to himself through Christ and gave us the ministry of reconciliation: that God was reconciling the world to himself in Christ, not counting people's sins against them. And he has committed to us the message of reconciliation. We are therefore, Christ's ambassadors, as though God were making his appeal through us. We implore you on Christ's behalf: Be reconciled to God. God made him who had no sin to be sin for us so that in him we might become the righteousness of God."

Did you catch that? We are Christ ambassadors. It is our job, as believers in a church body, to help those who have fallen and repented. Stop making fear-based decisions and start making faith-based decisions. No Christian hurts worse than one who has committed a deep sin and, instead of restoration, has been rejected. How can we then proclaim God forgives all? Yes, he does, but the forgiveness of Christ needs to be displayed through us. We shouldn't put ourselves on a pedestal, believing our sins are not as bad as our neighbors. We shouldn't think to ourselves, *I can't believe he did that. I would never do that. I sin, but not like he did.*

"These six things does the LORD hate: yea, seven are an abomination unto him: A proud look, a lying tongue, and hands that shed innocent blood, An heart that deviseth wicked imaginations, feet that be swift in running to mischief, A false witness that speaketh lies, and he that soweth discord among brethren."

— Proverbs 6:16–19, (KJV)

The above scripture often surprises a lot of people. But it really puts things into perspective, doesn't it? God puts a prideful person on the same plane as one who murders an innocent person and someone who quickly runs into trouble on the same level as someone who lies. That sure is different than our way of thinking, isn't it? *We have a hard time forgiving believers who have sinned because we don't see our sin the way God sees it.* We excuse ourselves for the way we behave but refuse to forgive those around us. If we really looked in the mirror and examined ourselves, we would see ourselves as sinners who have been saved by grace through faith. Nothing more. Nothing less.

We need to stop thinking as a church (the body of believers) that when someone has sinned grievously, it means they were never truly saved or they cannot have the Holy Spirit within them. This simply isn't true. When a person harbors resentment and fails to ask for forgiveness, the Bible warns that it can grow like a tree inside them. Hebrews 12:15 (NASB) says, "See to it that no one comes short of the grace of God; that no root of bitterness springing up causes trouble, and by it, many become defiled."

In my practice, I have observed several traits that seem to be common to those who commit horrendous sins:

1. They have grown bitter toward someone or about a situation.

2. They do not have a love relationship with the Lord through prayer. Sometimes, they are avid Bible readers but do not trust the Lord to take care of the situation in their lives, so bitterness festers.

3. They refuse to open up to others. Often, because we don't see the church dealing with people's sins, we fear

rejection if we tell others what is happening in our lives. I will elaborate on this topic later.

4. The Bible says that Satan is as fierce as a lion. "Be alert and of sober mind. Your enemy, the devil, prowls around like a roaring lion looking for someone to devour." (I Peter 5:8 NIV). Resist him, standing firm in the faith, because you know that the family of believers throughout the world is undergoing the same kind of suffering. We don't take Satan and his temptations seriously enough. We don't flee temptation. "Do not enter the path of the wicked And do not proceed in the way of evil people." (Proverbs 4:14, NASB). That's pretty definitive. Get out of the situation. Open up to someone. Get your mind and body into positive thoughts and behaviors. Review the pizza illustration in Chapter five.

Reconciliation will give you more peace and joy than you ever imagined. There are so many hurting people in this world who have experienced rejection from Christians and have turned away from the church because they feel that Christ has also rejected them. Reconciliation takes time because our flesh does not want to deal with people's sins, especially if the sin is horrible and we can no longer trust the person. It will take much prayer and effort to put songs and bible verses that you know into actual practice.

God takes reconciliation very seriously. Matthew 5:23–24 (ESV) talks about presenting your offering to the Lord. "So if you are offering your gift at the altar and there remember that your brother has something against you, leave your gift there before the altar and go. First be reconciled to your brother, and then come and offer your gift." Either we put God's Word into practice, or we decide to forget what we see when we look in a mirror. See James1:23–27. If you are having a hard time with this, ask for help from someone who knows the scripture, not someone who will exacerbate your fears.

Forgiving those who have sinned and loving them back into the fellowship of believers is one of the best examples of Christianity. To not only forgive a fallen believer but also to help restore him to fellowship is a beautiful characteristic of the committed Christian. Plus, it is also a great testimony to his family, who might or might not be believers. Unfortunately, in over 30 years of counseling, I have seen *unbelievers* who are better at this than *believers*. They often say, "Who am I to judge? I have done plenty of sinning, so how can I not forgive their sins?"

Many Christians live a great life and have been following the Lord for several years. Therefore, they don't see their sins as significant. Because of this, they cannot conceive falling away from God. This belief leads to a total disconnect from the Ministry of Reconciliation. This type of person avoids those who anger them. They want those who have disappointed them to be constantly reminded of what they have done and often wish the offender would withdraw from church activities. This is why having a solid restoration ministry and utilizing believers to help those facing a crisis is a much-needed service.

Having a restoration program in a church would also provide those victims with Biblical counseling. They would then feel confident in the church's desire to help both the offender and the offended. It's important to understand that people who have sinned grievously and repented are a great resource for those who are struggling with unforgiveness. We need, as a body of believers, to start talking about restoration. We need to understand that people who carry around unforgiveness are not only giving into fear but also have the root of bitterness inside their hearts.

Hebrews 12:15 (NIV) says, "See to it that no one falls short of the grace of God and that no bitter root grows up to cause trouble and defile many." When you let unforgiveness take root and refuse to reconcile with a repentant believer, it grows inside you and will defile your soul. Even though by the grace of God, eternal life is secured once we trust Christ as our Savior, you can live a joyless life if you harden your heart toward others.

Not only will bitterness rob your joy in Christ, but it will also cause you to lose effectiveness as a witness. When you're joyful, your spirit attracts people, and they wonder how they, too, can have a life full of joy. Joy is not the same as happiness. It's easy to feel happy when things are going well, but joy is peace in the midst of life's circumstances. When you have joy, you have peace because you know the Lord is in control, and He will never give you more than you can handle.

> "My grace is sufficient for thee: for my strength is made perfect in weakness."
>
> —2 Corinthians 12:9 (KJV)

Refusing to recognize a believer's repentance and redemption is the same as doubting Jesus' ability to heal completely. It is spitting in the face of Jesus and refusing to accept the fact that when a person repents, they are wiped clean by the grace of God. "Then I acknowledged my sin to you and did not cover up my iniquity. I said, 'I will confess my transgressions to the LORD.' And you forgave the guilt of my sin.'" (Psalm 32:5 (NIV)

Did Jesus heal the man of blindness only for him to become blind later on? Or did He heal him completely? How about the man He healed of leprosy, or Lazarus, who He raised from the dead? When a believer sins grievously, the first thing he needs to do is repent and receive the forgiveness of Christ. Then, he needs to make amends and go through the church's restoration program. Do we, as believers, have the right to withhold forgiveness and reconciliation? Do we have the right to make sure the person stays in bondage to their sin? If we refuse to exercise the ministry of reconciliation, we will be robbed of our joy.

Have you ever heard of Scriptural separation? I have never heard it preached, nor do I know many counselors that use this scriptural principle. I Corinthians 7:10–11 (NKJV) says, "Now to the married I command, yet not I but the Lord: A wife is not to depart from her husband. But even if she does depart, let her remain unmarried or be reconciled to *her* husband. And a husband is not to divorce *his* wife."

Let's break this passage down:

This passage is not talking about someone who is married to an unbeliever. We will delve into that next. The above passage talks about *believers* who are married to one another.

1. It is not a passive action; you separate, but the goal is reconciliation whenever possible. It requires seeking both individual and couples counseling. It requires honesty about each individual's part in the marital problems.

2. You are not adding any more issues or stress to the marriage. Instead, you are focused on building a Christ-centered home, not just for yourselves but also for your children.

Scriptural separation actually prevents divorce. However, many pastors do not preach I Corinthians 7:10–11 because they believe people will divorce in droves. The opposite is true. A lot of believers do not even seek counseling before they seek a divorce. They have *given up* and see no other way. The counseling goal is for both parties to repent of their actions, ask for forgiveness, and work toward a healthy partnership.

Divorce should be the last resort. Christian couples should first seek Biblical counseling when trying to resolve their issues. Divorce is a decisive step that should not be taken lightly. When is this appropriate? In the case of physical, emotional, sexual abuse, or adultery. There are too many Christians living with substance abusers or other forms of abuse who don't seek guidance from the church and remain stuck hiding their situation.

If a separation occurs, remain single. Now is not the time to start dating other people. You are in a spiritual battle, and you need to get your sword—the Word of God to help you through it. By staying single, you will be able to show your partner your commitment to working out the marital problems.

There was a woman who wanted to separate from her husband for a short time. Her counselor, however, vehemently opposed her decision. A few months later, her husband asked for a divorce and refused to attend couples counseling or try any other steps to save the marriage. Ten years later, she still believes a trial separation would have helped save her marriage.

One thing I was taught very early on in my counseling career was never to let anybody leave my office feeling hopeless. When people feel hopeless and stop caring about their lives, they are more likely to engage in behaviors they wouldn't normally consider. *An unhappy couple + isolation + an unwillingness to confront issues = potentially disastrous results.* Marriages where one or both parties are not fully committed lead to feelings of hopelessness, despondency, depression, and helplessness.

I will give you an example. There was a young couple in the church I attended. The husband was constantly drinking. The wife, desperate for a solution, tried both individual and couples counseling to no avail. When I counseled the wife, she and I discussed the possibility of a temporary separation. She decided to leave. Three weeks later, they were back in my office. He said, "Telling her to leave was the best thing that you could have done. When I walked into the empty house, it hit me. I was substituting the bottle for my family. Nothing else would have impacted me like that." I continued counseling them for a while to address some underlying issues, and eventually, they reconciled. They are still together.

I was married for 27 years. It was an extremely unhappy marriage. There was a lot of abuse in the home. I wish I had separated years before I did, but I felt stuck. I kept hearing that if I worked hard enough, the marriage would improve. I'm not going to say I did everything right, but I tried, even when my children wanted me to leave. When I finally separated, my daughter called to tell me my husband was dating. It was a shock. The next thing I knew, he wanted a divorce. He remarried three days after our divorce was finalized.

Divorce is the chance you take when you decide to separate. Your spouse might not be willing to do the work to fix the marriage and may even choose to *move on,* as mine did. But staying because you *don't want to be divorced* is not the answer. Plus, if your spouse decides to seek a divorce, they can do it against your will. Only Christ can change a person's heart, but they have to want to have their heart changed.

On the other hand, a separation can provide alone time with the Lord. When we are open to God's guidance, He can show us things in life that may not have been examined before and help us to reach the goal of reconciling and forming a whole and healthy unit. What are some of the ramifications if separation is not taught in the local church?

- Christians get discouraged about all the issues in their marriage and get divorced without getting counseling. I'm always surprised by this because it applies not only to the laity but also to heads of ministry, pastors, Sunday school teachers, and Bible college professors. It is hard to believe, but most of these people have attended church all their adult lives, and yet they believe there is no way out of their situation, so they decide to divorce without even seeking counseling.

- As I mentioned previously, I was taught never to let a person leave my office feeling hopeless. When people feel hopeless, they do crazy things. Suicide, adultery, molestation, drunkenness, and drug abuse are just a few. You name it, Christians have done it. It is hard for many to think a Christian can do these things, but being in a hopeless situation or feeling trapped leads many to commit sins they never dreamed of doing. We need to encourage people to reach out to Bible-believing counselors and those who will provide encouragement and hope. There is always hope. You may think a Christian could never commit such sins, but Satan will use hopelessness as a means to control and manipulate. Afterward, Christians will often say, "I can't believe I did that," since the behavior is not a pattern but a desperate cry for help.

- Individuals will stay in a marriage but will not work on the marriage or themselves. Instead, they will get involved in other activities, which may seem healthy but isn't because they are not dealing with their problems. They are avoiding. As Henry David Thoreau would say, "they are living lives of quiet desperation and go to the grave with the song still in them." Jesus wants us to really live. "I am come that they may have life, and that they may have it more abundantly." John 10:10 (KJV)

I have heard Malachi 2:16 (NLT) quoted as "God hates divorce." Yes, He does. God hates all sin, but as a church, we must recognize that some couples are in abusive relationships, and the church often fails to offer help. Sometimes, additional hurt is caused when couples are not told about spiritual separation, which can allow time for healing.

In some cases, one partner may quickly move

on to a new relationship without any desire to restore the marriage. While it only takes one person to break a marriage, it requires both parties to work on the relationship and have the marriage God intended. A marriage that honors Him and draws others to Christ by the love they show to each other. If you are in a very troubled marriage, it is hard to draw people to Christ since your misery can show outwardly.

The unique bond between husband and wife is meant to help each person grow in their communion with Christ. It is a complementary relationship. They can see each other's strengths and needs and help each other become more Christ-like in their walk. If this is not your marriage, it can be! With God, all things are possible. But it will take commitment from both partners. "If God is for us, who can be against us?" (Romans 8:31, NIV).

I Corinthians 7:13–14 (KJV) states, "And the woman which hath an husband that believeth not, and if he be pleased to dwell with her, let her not leave him. For the unbelieving husband is sanctified by the wife, and the unbelieving wife is sanctified by the husband: else were your children unclean; but now are they holy." I have heard many pastors talk about the believing spouse staying with an unbeliever, but I have never heard them mention the portion about him being please to dwell with her. What does it mean? Think about when you are happy being with someone. You want to do things with them, make them happy, and enjoy their company. It is not merely existing together. It is the same word in Acts 8:1 that is used for hearty agreement. It is not merely existing together but actually trying to build a life together.

I know a lot of couples that are living together-miserably. They think they are pleasing God. by staying together, but Jesus wants us to work on our marriage. It is supposed to be a picture of the bride of Christ and to draw others to Christ. So, if you are in an abusive relationship, get out. I'm not saying divorce; I'm saying remove yourself from the situation and trust God to show you the way through. How much is your mental health worth? It is certainly worth more than the trappings of the world.

Many Christians are waiting for the magical God to show up. They pray that God will wave a magic wand and heal their marriage or fix their circumstances. They say God wants them to be happy. But God often doesn't do the things He has empowered *us* to do. He wants us to have an abundant life. Joy through Him. God wants us to be happy. God's goal for us is to be Christ-like, and by working toward this goal, you will find joy. What is the difference between joy and happiness? Joy is peace in the midst of the circumstances, while happiness is what the world has when everything is going your way.

Working on a marriage is not an easy task but it does take two people. So, if you decide to separate, you must remain committed to working on your marriage even if your spouse is not joining you in the process. You must also use the time to work on yourself and your relationship with Jesus Christ. It may mean being single for the rest of your life. I don't know. But it does require daily trust that God will heal you, your spouse, and your children, who have surely suffered from the circumstances.

I have counseled many people, and I will tell you that children whose parents have a good relationship and love each other tend to do better in life, even if one or both parents are unsaved. That is why, instead of focusing on the mechanics of rearing a child, parents should focus on their marital relationship and make it an example of Christ loving the church.

God is a loving Father, but sometimes people have a very skewed vision of Him because they don't remember their dad as someone they admire or who loved them unconditionally. It is often tough to get past this and to see God has a loving father. Also, females often subconsciously choose a man who is like their dad. That should be a sobering thought for any man who has a daughter!

This answers the question often presented: "How could she marry an alcoholic after what she went through with her dad? I can't believe how her husband talks to her and how abusive he is. Why does she put up with it?" The same situation goes for men. They might have had a very controlling, domineering mother and then subconsciously repeat the pattern in their marriage.

This topic brings me to one of my greatest joys: premarital counseling. I see it as one of the pivotal ministries in the church. It can save a couple from making a big mistake and also save the lives of future children. My two biggest pet peeves about premarital counseling in the church are:

1. It is not taken seriously enough. I feel

that as soon as a couple is engaged, they should have to go through six weeks of premarital counseling. If counseling is done too late in the engagement, it may be difficult for a couple to break it off if a real problem comes up because too many plans may already be in place. The church should refuse to marry a couple if they have not gone through the program, even if they are on the church staff. You would be surprised at how many underlying issues many couples do not think about or hide before getting married.

2. The program should encompass a questionnaire that includes questions about faith, what it means to the individuals and its place in their lives. Has the couple put aside time for devotions together? Have they addressed their finances? How does their family of origin think about money? How will they deal with anger and problems that will arise? What is their sexual history? Is there honesty between the couple?

These are just a few of the topics which should be covered. Premarital counseling is time-consuming; therefore, seek a Biblical counselor who has a comprehensive program.

Pastors are responsible to the Lord for who they unite in marriage and should take the task very seriously. Simply because two people know the Lord does not mean God has chosen for them to be partners. In fact, when I took a class about conducting premarital counseling, I was told when done correctly, 60% of people will decide not to get married! That is an astonishing figure! With that number in mind, I fear the reason we don't see more broken engagements is because premarital counseling is not hitting the complex issues and is being conducted too late in the engagement. Timing is pivotal since a wedding is a significant expense, and many go through with the marriage because they feel guilty about the money that has been spent. Note to parents: Your child's happiness is of much greater importance than money. If you see they are having doubts, encourage them to talk to you.

A wedding is over in one day! Yet, a lot of

Christian couples get caught up with the world's view of a wedding and spend outrageous sums of money. Perspective is often lost when planning. It's important to remember the Lord cares about all the things in our lives, and He will help us plan wisely if we ask His guidance in being good stewards of our money.

Good premarital counseling, marriage counseling, and separation are some of the tools that help prevent divorce, but they are not guarantees. There are many situations that, if left unaddressed and continue can ultimately cause a breakup. Remember, the Lord has forgiven, and we are responsible for a ministry of reconciliation, but it must start with a repentant sinner. These are some behaviors that can break a marriage

- A lack of repentance
- An unfaithful spouse
- An abusive spouse
- An unbeliever who does not want to live with their spouse

The church has to recognize that these are foundations for divorce, and divorced people should not be classified as less than acceptable saints.

Remember, after David's sin with Bathsheba, followed by having her husband killed, the Lord still allowed him to maintain his kingship because of his repentance. However, there were dire consequences as a result of his sin. Read II Samuel 11–12. Sometimes, the church extends the consequences of believers' sin by refusing to allow them to serve in ministries in the church for fear of what others in the congregation might say. Instead of wishing those who have sinned grievously to leave, the church body should be looking at ways they can use the testimony of people who still want their lives to count for Christ.

I often wonder what would have happened if Moses had repented for striking the rock instead of speaking to it when getting water for the people (Numbers 20:11). Would he have been allowed to see the promised land? Unfortunately, scripture reveals that even in his last days, Moses didn't repent for his behavior and blamed the people for being unruly and quarrelsome.

7
FINANCES

We touched a little on finances in the previous chapter when talking about weddings, but the Bible says a lot about how we should handle money. Being a good steward of money is pleasing to the Lord. Unfortunately, most Christians do not have this discipline. They are still on the world's hamster wheel, trying to obtain as many possessions as they can, and are not taking a Biblical attitude toward spending.

Tithing:

Let's talk about tithing. First of all, there is a significant distinction between the Old Covenant (Old Testament) and the New Covenant (New Testament) in the scriptures. The Old Testament concerns the law. When it comes to tithing, the Old Testament is clear. Numbers 18:26 (NIV) states, "'Speak to the Levites and say to them: 'When you receive from the Israelites the tithe I give you as your inheritance, you must present a tenth of that tithe as the LORD's offering.'" It's pretty simplistic. Give a tenth of what God has given you, and as you are further blessed, offer additional gifts. In the New Testament or Covenant, Matthew 23:23 (NIV) describes what Jesus says about tithing: "Woe to you, teachers of the law and Pharisees, you hypocrites! You give a tenth of your spices—mint, dill, and cumin. But you have neglected the more important matters of the law—justice, mercy, and faithfulness. You should have practiced the latter without neglecting the former." In other words, our lives should be in balance. We should be displaying grace and mercy while supporting God's work through the blessings God has given us.

The New Covenant is always about grace verses the law. For example, "You shall not murder." (Exodus 20:13, NIV). Okay, that's nice and clear. I can handle that. Then there is the New Testament I John 3:15 (KJV), "Whosoever hateth his brother is a murderer: and ye know that no murderer hath eternal life abiding in him." Have I had hatred in my heart towards someone? Yes, I have. Does that mean I don't have eternal life? No. If you accept Christ as your Savior, *all* your sins, past, present, and future, are buried at the cross.

Hebrews 8:6 (ESV) explains, "But as it is, Christ has obtained a ministry that is much more excellent than the old as the covenant he mediates is better since it is enacted on better promises." So, how can I not hate my brother? By being in God's Word every day, seeking to strengthen my walk with Christ, and asking the Lord to help me love as he loved and forgive as he forgave.

What does this have to do with tithing? Everything! Just as God says not to commit adultery Old Covenant (Exodus 20:14), the New Covenant says not to even look at someone with lust (Matthew 5:28). Which is harder to do? So when it comes to tithing, if we follow the Old Testament, we would give $1,000 for every $10,000 earned, but when following the New Testament, if we earn $10,000 but feel incredibly blessed, we might decide to give $5,000. Do you see the difference? It's about heart and blessings rather than responsibility.

Many churches hang onto the Old Covenant, "You must set aside a tithe of your crops—one-tenth of all the crops you harvest each year." (Deuteronomy 14:22, NLT). Whereas the New Covenant reads, "Remember this: Whoever sows sparingly will reap sparingly, and whoever sows generously will reap generously. Each of you should give what you have decided in your heart to give, not reluctantly or under compulsion, for God loves a cheerful giver." (II Corinthians 9:6–7, NIV).

So how should you give? Figure out what you made to the penny and give 10% or give cheerfully just as God has blessed you. The Lord has greatly blessed me. He wants me to give because I love Him and want to be a part of His ministry, not because I feel obligated.

> "But whoso hath this world's good, and seeth his brother have need, and shutteth up his bowels of compassion from him, how dwelleth the love of God in him?"
>
> —I John 3:17, KJV

> "Beloved, thou doest faithfully whatsoever thou doest to the brethren, and to strangers; Which have borne witness of thy charity before the church: whom if thou bring forward on their journey after a godly sort, thou shalt do

well: Because that for his name's sake they went forth, taking nothing of the Gentiles. We therefore ought to receive such, that we might be fellow helpers to the truth."

—III John 5-8, KJV

"Lay not up for yourselves treasures upon earth, where moth and rust doth corrupt, and where thieves break through and steal: But lay up for yourselves treasures in heaven, where neither moth nor rust doth corrupt, and where thieves do not break through nor steal: For where your treasure is, there will your heart be also."

—Matthew 6:19-21 KJV

God sees all we do, and it's our job to provide for the ministries that bring others to Christ. Christians should be careful with their giving since there are so many needs in the world. Remember, the hungry can be given food and a homeless shelter, but they also need to hear the love of God and

Jesus' payment on the cross for their sins. The homeless need a place to stay, but their most urgent need is to hear about God's love. Familiarize yourself with the ministers you give to. They should wisely use the money and reach out to others with the gospel while fulfilling the specified need.

Do you want to be blessed financially? Then, be a good steward of the money God gives you. Be a cheerful giver. Give to ministries that are reaching others with the gospel and teaching the Word of God. You cannot outgive God. He promises that in His word. So use the money God gives you wisely. You might not have the latest fashions or the newest cars, but contentment comes with spending and giving in ways that are pleasing to the Lord.

Stepping out in faith and trusting in what God will do with your life doesn't mean God does not want you to have nice things; it means you are weighing your spending with the treasures you are building up in heaven. "Call unto Me, and I will answer you, and show you great and mighty things, which you do not know." (Jeremiah 33:3, NKJV)

If we are confident that God will provide for

our needs, should we ask for money? In prayer, yes. Between you and the Lord. I once heard an interesting story about a missionary who was translating the Bible and hired a native to help him. After several months, the missionary asked the man if he would like to become a Christian. The man responded, "I think I would if I would meet one someday." Confused, the missionary asked, " What do you mean?" "Well," the man replied, "I have been around this mission for several years. People are constantly talking about how Christ takes care of them and meets their needs, but all they talk about is their need for money." Sobering, isn't it? God has many ways to give you money and to take away money. Our job is to be faithful.

We should follow the example of George Muller, a missionary who ran the Ashley Down orphanage in Bristol, England. He determined early on that he would never ask for money but would pray about his needs and let the Lord take care of him. He stayed true to his promise, and in his lifetime, millions of dollars passed through his hands.

Ministries need money to do God's work, and God is able to provide cash in many ways. He can use anyone, including the unsaved, to support

His ministries. His work comes in many forms. For example, there was a pastor in Nashville who bought a building in the middle of the city and was blessed when, a couple of months later, an organization approached him to rent some of the space. It was completely unexpected and a great help to the Church. God promises that He will bless His people when we give willingly and with a cheerful heart.

> "'Yours, LORD, is the greatness and the power and the glory and the majesty and the splendor, for everything in heaven and earth is yours. Yours, LORD, is the kingdom; you are exalted as head over all. Wealth and honor come from you; you are the ruler of all things. In your hands are strength and power to exalt and give strength to all. Now, our God, we give you thanks, and praise your glorious name. 'But who am I, and who are my people, that we should be able to give as generously as this? Everything comes from you, and we have given you only what comes

from your hand.'"

—I Chronicles 29:11–14, (NIV)

Did you catch that? They were overjoyed with the privilege of giving to God. All the wealth we accumulate is from the Lord. He gives us the ability to earn money, and it's our responsibility to use His money wisely and give with a cheerful heart. I Timothy 5:17–18 (ESV) tells us to "'Let the elders who rule well be considered worthy of double honor, especially those who labor in preaching and teaching. For the Scripture says, 'You shall not muzzle an ox when it treads out the grain,' and 'The laborer deserves his wages.'" Look at the people in full-time Christian ministry. Are they faithful to God's word? Are they sacrificing for the ministry? Pray about their needs and see where you fit in to bless them.

> "We ought therefore to show hospitality to such people so that we may work together for the truth."
>
> —III John 8, (NIV)

Showing Hospitality:

Showing hospitality means giving of yourself. It means possibly having a Christian school teacher over for dinner. Having guests in your home is a lost art these days. The gift of hospitality is about being welcoming to others and concentrating on the fellowship you will have together. It's not about showcasing your home. You don't have to slave over the stove to prepare a meal. Make it easy and fun so you can spend more time with your guests. Opening your home and heart to others in need can change your life.

Giving of your gifts and talents:

Frequently, we ignore our unique talents as a means to share God's Word with others. The world takes it seriously when a person makes a deathbed confession. It's assumed a person is sharing his deepest truth and would not lie before his death. So, shouldn't we take Jesus' last words to his disciples before he ascended to heaven as seriously? Jesus tells us in Acts 1:8 (NIV), "Buy you will receive power when the Holy Spirit comes on you, and you will be my witnesses in Jerusalem, and in all Judea and Samaria, and to the end of the earth."

What a powerful statement! But do we heed the message? God is commanding us to tell others, and He will equip us with the ability to share His word. I recommend *Moments With The Book* they have an excellent tract ministry. The tracts are easy to use, even with a busy schedule. Plus, it's a great way to show how much Jesus loves and cares for us. In these difficult times, people want to know the truth.

God will always provide the tools needed to accomplish what He wants in your life. If you pray for God to equip you to become a giver, He will reveal to you the needs around you. If you want to be a witness, He will provide the opportunities wherever you go.

Two principles to help encourage you as a witness:

1. People hated Jesus, who was God's perfect son. So, we should not get upset when people dislike us for sharing His Word. It's not about you. It's about doing what is pleasing to the Lord and knowing that He sees your heart.

2. The world needs Christ. Imagine if everyone in the world suddenly got cancer, but you had a cure. Would you interrupt their lives to tell them about it? Even when someone seems to have it all together, they might be miserable inside, searching for a solution. Jesus is the answer.

My challenge to those supporting church ministry:

Pastors:

Teach your congregation to spend time daily with the Lord, reading the scriptures. Instruct them on the Word, verse-by-verse and chapter-by-chapter. When Christians fall in love with the Lord they want to be obedient in all aspects of the Christian Walk. Examine your church's needs and pray about them. Focus on aligning the church with Christ's mission on earth. Trust Him to provide.

Christians:

Trust in the Lord. He will provide for your needs. Philippians 4:19 (NASB) says, "And my God will supply all your needs according to His riches in glory in Christ Jesus." How rich do you think Jesus is? Measureless. He owns everything in the world. His resources are endless.

Don't spend all your time focused on obtaining more riches. Examine your spending and be intentional with what God has given you. Be a cheerful giver and contribute what you can to the furthering of Christ's gospel.

Does being a giver guarantee that you will not suffer pain? Does it guarantee God will protect you from tragedy and sadness? There is no better place to find the answer than in Job 1. Job was a very wealthy man. He was perfect, upright, feared God, and avoided evil. One day, Satan and God have a conversation. Satan tells God that Job is only faithful because God has built a hedge of protection around him. To our amazement, God gives Satan permission (notice the word permission) to take away everything Job has, including all his worldly possessions and his ten children. Still, Job remains faithful.

As we read on, we see that Satan is still dissatisfied. He wants to destroy Job the same way he longs to destroy all Christians. God then allows Satan to hurt Job physically, but he is forbidden from killing him. Again, Job continues to be faithful regardless of his circumstances. What a testimony!

Job's story is a true testimony for us. God was still God when Job had all his worldly possessions, and He remained Job's God when Satan took everything away. If Christians never experienced pain in their lives, they wouldn't be able to help others in pain. It's through the fire that faith grows stronger.

I said earlier to take notice of the word permission. It is an important word in Job. Note that God *permits* Satan to harm Job. Satan cannot do anything to us unless God allows it. A lot of Christians think giving and faithfulness shield them from trouble, since God provides us with guardian angels (Hebrews 1:14). Still, that does not mean He will not allow difficulties into our lives. However, God does make a promise in Romans 8:28 (KJV), "And we know that all things work together for good to them that love God, to them who are the called according to his purpose." Sin brings trouble in our lives, yet He is merciful and sometimes does not punish us as harshly as we deserve.

If we remain faithful, we may be spared the consequences of behaviors that displease God. For instance, by choosing to eat healthy and taking care of yourself, you may avoid certain diseases and remain more vibrant for God's work. Just think: Noah was 500 years old when he started building the ark. Stay in shape! You never know what God will ask you to do when you're 500 years old!

A Giving Recap:

1. Ask God how to use the money, gifts, and talents he has bestowed upon you.
2. Search for ministries and people that you would consider supporting. Ask yourself which ministries provide for your and your family's needs.
3. Give abundantly and cheerfully–10% may mean nothing to you. You cannot outgive God. He has plenty of ways to provide for you.

4. Examine your output. Do you eat a lot when you go out? Stay in instead. Why not get the family involved with prep time and pre-planning? It is easy to eat right when you pre-plan and have ingredients available. Having supplies allows you the flexibility of putting a meal together quickly if you must. Do you need to have the latest fashions, the newest cars, or the most prominent house? Let God show you the best ways to make and save money. You will be surprised at how much you might be able to give.

5. It is a joy to be involved in ministry. Don't ever forget that. God is pleased when we give, and He knows our hearts. You will reap what you sow. "And let us not be weary in well doing: for in due season we shall reap if we faint not." (Galatians 6:9, KJV). Most of the time, reaping what you sow is put into a bad connotation, but that misses the double meaning. If you sow good deeds, God promises *in*

due time, you will reap good benefits. A lot of people are sowing beets and are surprised when they harvest corn. I have nothing against beets, but they can't hold a candle to a wonderful ear of corn.

6. If you are always on the short end of the stick when it comes to money, consider the reason that you have not been blessed in this area. Analyze your budget. Is a need for validation causing you to overspend? Are you buying things as a substitution for the fulfillment you can have in Christ? Spend TAG (time alone with God) immersed in His Word and prayer for victory. You will experience what it is like to have the mind of Christ and have a desire to lay up your treasures in heaven.

7. How are you currently taking care of the blessings God has given you? Are you trying to be the best employee you can be, even when it isn't your dream job? Are you presently taking

care of the things that you have? Luke 16:10 (AMP) says, "He who is faithful in a very little thing is also faithful in much; and he who is dishonest in a very little thing is also dishonest in much." Be grateful for what you have and share with others using the talents and blessings God has given you.

8
UNCONDITIONAL LOVE

Unconditional love is a term that many of us take for granted. The truth is it's rare. When I was working in foster care, I was astounded to discover the number of children who did not have someone to love them unconditionally. What is unconditional love?

God loves us so much that he sent His only Son to die for us. We've all heard that fact before, but because we've listened to it so often, it can lose its impact. Why did God do this? Hebrews 9:22 (ESV) reads, "Indeed, under the law almost everything is purified with blood, and without the shedding of blood there is no forgiveness of sins." Why is this? Most of us can recall our parents saying, "Because I said so." The same is true with God. Blood is required to forgive sins because God said so.

In the Old Testament, blood sacrifices occurred daily, and the high priest would perform a yearly sacrifice for all sins–including his. Catch that.

The high priest needed to make a sacrifice for his own sins because he was not sinless. Jesus, however, did not need a sacrifice for himself. He was absolutely God and absolutely sinless. Hebrews 9:14 (NIV) reads, "How much more, then, will the blood of Christ, who through the eternal Spirit offered himself unblemished to God, cleanse our consciences from acts that lead to death, so that we may serve the living God!" Jesus was unblemished. He was perfect, and he offered himself; no one dragged Jesus to the cross.

Jesus gave up His life for us. In Matthew 26:53 (NIV), Jesus says, "Do you think I cannot call on my Father, and he will at once put at my disposal more than twelve legions of angels." Twelve legions of angels are 72,000, give or take a few thousand. It is hard for us to fathom how much pain and suffering Jesus endured in the hours leading up to and including the crucifixion. *The Passion of the Christ* was heavily criticized for its depiction of violence. It was hard to watch. But, in truth, the movie only touches the surface of what Jesus really experienced." In the film, Jim Caviezel Jr., who played Jesus, was still recognizable, but the Bible states Jesus was disfigured beyond recognition. It is hard to comprehend!

"Just as there were many who were
appalled at him his appearance was
so disfigured beyond that of any
human being and his form marred
beyond human likeness."

—Isaiah 52:14, (NIV)

I recommend watching this film to all
Christians. Yes, it is incomprehensible to think of
what God allowed His son to go through for us.
Why? The most straightforward answer is that God
wanted to show us His unconditional love. No matter
what our sin is, without exception, it is forgiven at
the cross. The payment for blood was made. Even the
most evil person in history with the most egregious
sins is covered.

No one goes to hell because their sin was not
paid for. When Jesus died, he died for all. People go to
hell because they refuse to accept the payment Christ
made on the cross. Pride keeps so many people away
from heaven for eternity. They will not accept the fact
that their good works have nothing to do with getting
into heaven except for the excellent work of accepting
Christ's payment for sins at the cross.

Christ loves us *all* unconditionally, no matter the sin. He died for us all and works at bringing us to Him our entire lives. I have heard many unsaved people talk about their near-death experiences involving cancer, horrible accidents, and situations where doctors couldn't give them any hope. Yet, somehow, they are still here. I say to them, "I know why you are alive. God saved you so that I could tell you about Jesus and how much he loves you. He sent his son to die on the cross for your sins."

How is His love to be demonstrated in our lives? Once we have accepted Christ as our Savior, our lives should be Christ-like. But we cannot be Christ-like without Christ. You might be a good person, but that is not the same as accepting Christ. If you have not accepted Christ, let me stop right here. God has made it easy for us since it was excruciating for Him. Can you imagine letting your son sacrifice His life for someone who curses and hates Him? It is unimaginable. If you are just realizing the depth of Jesus' love for you, trust Him now. He would have gone to the cross even if you were the only one needing to be saved. You can accept Him as your Savior. Ask Him for forgiveness of your sins and thank him for His sacrifice.

Does it seem too easy? Let's look at the thief on the cross. Two thieves were being crucified with Jesus. In Luke 23:39 (NIV), the Bible records one thief saying, "Aren't you the Messiah? Save yourself and us!" but Luke 23:40–43 (NIV) says, "But the other criminal rebuked him, 'Don't you fear God, since you are under the same sentence? We are punished justly, for we are getting what our deeds deserve, but this man has done nothing wrong.' Then he said, 'Jesus, remember me when you come into your kingdom.' Jesus answered him, 'Truly I tell you, today you will be with me in paradise.'"

Why was the second man able to live with Christ for eternity? Did he get down from the cross and get baptized? Did he go to church? Did he do any good deeds that deserved eternal life? None of these. He believed that Jesus was God the Messiah (meaning a leader or savior) and had the power to bring him into His eternal kingdom. This story is one of the most powerful examples, clearly showing us that our good works don't save us. Only recognizing Jesus is God who came to earth to die for our sins saves us. Jesus did many good works while he was on Earth, but He did not come to Earth to *show us the way to live a good life.* He came to die for us.

Now that we have Christ as our Savior, what do we do with this newfound faith? This question is the reason I wrote this book. I want to share basic knowledge and create a thirst for God's word in believers. When you start falling in love with Christ and His Word, you will want to share Him with those around you. You will want to tell others of His unconditional love. When I see Christians who do not have any burden to tell others about Jesus, I wonder if they are genuinely in love with Him.

Remember when you were first in love and couldn't wait to tell others all about the person you loved? Your friends didn't have to wonder because you were eager to share your love story. That is how it is when you start reading God's word. As you delve deeper into the Word and learn about His workings in people's lives, you long for an opening to talk about Jesus. Little by little, Jesus will become number one in your life. Everyone and everything else will be second to Him. Knowing Christ's suffering on the cross helps us to bear rejection from others. The world hated Jesus, and he was perfect, so it's logical to expect some people's resistance to the gospel. So what? Those individuals are not rejecting us as messengers; they are rejecting our precious Savior.

How do I get this love? Ask the Lord to love people through you. He loves the unlovely. It is easy to love people who are *your kind of people*. It is hard when they are not. It's especially tough when you know someone has sinned grievously. How do we handle that? We start seeing our sin as God sees it. Proverbs 6:16–19 (NIV) is really sobering. It reads, "There are six things the LORD hates, seven that are detestable to him: haughty eyes, a lying tongue, hands that shed innocent blood, a heart that devises wicked schemes, feet that are quick to rush into evil, a false witness who pours out lies and a person who stirs up conflict in the community." As you can see, God puts being proud (haughty eyes), lying, shedding innocent blood, and stirring up conflict all on the same level. All of us are guilty of some of these.

When we think, *I wouldn't have done what he did*, we are putting levels of sin that God does not. You might not have done what he did, but you will do something else. You also don't know the person's emotional and mental state or background, which may have driven them to sin. Only one percent of murderers are serial killers. Most people can trace their sin to a buildup of anger and resentment, which led to self-isolation and a reluctance to share what was happening in their lives.

So why do we find it so hard to demonstrate unconditional love in the church family? Why do we separate ourselves from those who are hurting from their past? The bottom line is that we have adopted the world's view of believing some people cannot be changed and that there is no help for them, along with the belief that Christians don't commit *those kinds of sins.*

These beliefs are wrong. Jeremiah 17:9 (KJV) tells us, "The heart is deceitful above all things, and desperately wicked: who can know it?" *All* of us are capable of deep sin. It is only through the grace of God, staying faithful in prayer, studying His Word, having fellowship with other believers, being involved in ministry, and sharing with others that we can prevent ourselves from falling into temptation. As Christians, we need to put on our faith glasses, which involves gaining knowledge about the situation instead of putting on our worldview glasses. When we have our worldview glasses on, we often shun the person, which leads to a lack of understanding and increases fears and anxiety.

I Peter 5:8 (NIV) says, "Be alert and of sober mind. Your enemy the devil prowls around like a roaring lion looking for someone to devour." We do not think about this enough, which keeps Satan ecstatic. We have an enemy that is trying to destroy our Christian Walk, and when we ignore that, we become lax in our walk. Even Jesus took time to pray to God. We need to stay close to the Lord and pray for Him to give us strength for today.

The Christian Walk is one of determination. It is about being purposeful, reading God's word, and asking him for help with our weaknesses. The Lord wants you to live a Christ-like life, but it takes effort. Before you watch your favorite program, have you prayed? Have you spent a few minutes in God's Word? There is always time to do the things you really want to do. If you received an all-expense paid two-week vacation, would you find the time? The vacation won't change your life, but learning God's word and allowing him to change you will.

It's wrong to believe people can't be changed. There is a difference between people that can not be changed and people that will not be changed. The person has to desire God to change them. But He does not wave a magic wand, and voila! It is a long, complex, and painful road.

In order for change to happen, there must be repentance and then a close examination of one's thoughts and actions. A Biblical counselor can help. Next, you must plan and implement a new way of thinking and acting. Bitterness, anger, desire for revenge, and ill will toward others have no place in the Christian Walk. You might need to make amends to others by asking for forgiveness and doing as the Lord prompts you to do.

Jesus is in the life-changing business. He came to heal people. Sometimes physically, but mainly from the prison of sin. As Christians, when we hear of a fallen brother, the first thing we should do is ask the Lord how we can assist in healing and bringing them back to Christ. We need to radiate the unconditional love that we have received through Christ. What a difference that would make in our lives.

Unfortunately, we often don't see the blessing we receive by restoring a fallen brother. Instead, we focus on removing them from our lives. So many people say, "I forgive them, but I do not want anything to do with them?" Show me in scripture where that attitude was endorsed. Matthew 18:21–22 Jesus tells Peter to forgive his brother 70x7. In other words, keep forgiving. It's impossible to forgive in that way if we remove them from our lives.

Many people have never given or received unconditional love in their lives. The world has a lot of broken families. The Bible talks about this in Luke 12:51–53 (NIV), where Jesus describes how things will be before His coming, "Do you think I came to bring peace on earth? No, I tell you, but division. From now on there will be five in one family divided against each other, three against two and two against three. They will be divided, father against son and son against father, mother against daughter and daughter against mother, mother-in-law against daughter-in-law and daughter-in-law against mother-in-law."

If you are new to the scriptures, this verse might surprise you. I grew up thinking I would spend eternity in heaven. But that is not scriptural. In I Thessalonians 4:17 (KJV), we learn about the rapture, "Then we which are alive and remain shall be caught up together with them in the clouds, to meet the Lord in the air: and so shall we ever be with the

Lord." This is called the rapture. We don't know when it will occur. It could happen anytime. However, as things get darker and further away from the Lord's teachings, we can assume His return is closer.

Some say the rapture will occur during the tribulation. I encourage you to research this for yourself. The tribulation will be on earth and will be like nothing we have ever known. There will be earthquakes, famine, and pestilence. All the islands will fall into the sea. Think of that New Yorkers in Manhattan! A man will rise up promising peace, but after three and a half years, will reveal himself to be the antichrist. People will be forced into getting a number put on their foreheads or hands. Without the number, people will not be able to purchase or sell anything. The book of Revelations describes all that will happen.

The Bible tells us that after seven years, Jesus will return with the people who have passed away, and He will reign over the earth for 1,000 years. Then, the heavens and earth will be rolled up like a scroll, replaced with a new heaven and earth, and we will reign with Christ forever and ever on the new earth. Hallelujah! This is a very abbreviated version. Just enough to wet your appetite and encourage you to see for yourself what a magnificent God we have. Isn't God sending His only Son to die for our sins a wonderful example of unconditional love? If we choose to accept His payment for our sins, we will live with Him for eternity.

So getting back to Luke 12:51–53, we see that some of the problems with relationships are a sign of the times. The family unit used to stick together no matter what, but it's not that way anymore. Now, there are instances where grandparents cannot see their grandchildren because of differences in politics or faith. With the prevalence of social media, people are substituting genuine relationships with banter between strangers. We live in a world where many believe others are dying to know what they had for dinner last night, where they are going tonight, where they went on vacation, or what TV programs they are watching. People claim they don't have the time to read their Bibles or make a phone call, but then they are almost continually checking their social media feeds.

Social media has created a schism in relationships because people *hang out* on social media and are not developing social skills. A word to the wise: only people who really care about you want to know what your life is like.

9
EXAMINE YOUR LIFE

Christians still display behaviors that go against God's word but don't recognize it in their lives. However, they are able to point sin out in others and question *how someone could behave in such a way*. It's human nature.

II Corinthians 10:12 (NKJV) tells us, "For we dare not class ourselves or compare ourselves with those who commend themselves. But they, measuring themselves by themselves, and comparing themselves among themselves, are not wise." But this is what we do all the time! We look at the sins of others and say, "I would never do that!" This might be very true, but you will do something else.

By comparing ourselves with others, we are constantly trying to reach an unattainable goal. If you seek to have nicer, bigger, better things, there will always be someone who has more. Our contentment should be in Christ. II Corinthians 13:5 (NIV) says, "Examine yourselves to see whether you are in the faith; test yourselves." We should start with the basics. Have we really accepted Christ as our Savior? Too many people believe that because they go to a particular church, believe Jesus died on the cross, or have a father or grandfather who is a pastor, then they are Christians.

The Lord paints a good picture when He says in Matthew 7:21 (KJV), "Not everyone that saith unto me, Lord, Lord, shall enter into the kingdom of heaven; but he that doeth the will of my Father which is in heaven." So, what is the Father's will? In John 6:40 (NKJV), Jesus tells us what the Father's will is: "And this is the will of Him that sent Me, that everyone who sees the Son, and believes in Him may have everlasting life, and I will raise him up at the last day." It is not just believing that Jesus died on the cross but believing that the payment He made on the cross with his shed blood was for *you* and that payment was complete. There is nothing you can do to pay for your own salvation; Jesus has already paid the price.

Many people believe in God's salvation but cannot free themselves from the idea that there is nothing they can do to earn or pay for their salvation.

They believe they are saved by grace but kept through works. In other words, God needs help from us to secure our salvation. This is entirely false. Christ's payment was one time, all complete and available to all who believe.

When you accept Christ as your Savior, you are born into God's family. What did you have to do to be born into your family? You were born. The same is true for God's family. You are born into it by accepting Christ's complete payment on the cross.

Can you leave your family? In simple terms, no. You can change your name, stop contact, or move across the country, but you remain a part of your earthly family. However, suppose you have zero contact with your parents, and they win the lottery. Will you receive any benefit from your parent's windfall? Probably not. Will you be invited on the big family vacation? No. They might even write you out of their will since they don't even know where you are.

Let's compare this with being in the family of God. It takes work to be close to your earthly family and it takes work to be close to the Lord. You have to spend time with your family, let them know what's going on in your life, care about what's going on in theirs, know their background, their likes and dislikes, and enjoy being with them. The same applies to God's family.

How do we spend time with the Lord? We spend time reading and studying His word. So often, people are unsure of how to begin. They skip through the Bible or start somewhere in the middle, so there is no continuity of thought. My husband figured out that if you study daily and begin with Genesis in the Old Testament and Matthew in the New Testament, you will read the New Testament three times a year and the Old Testament once. I also like to read one or two chapters of Psalms (starting with the first chapter) and Proverbs each day. For example, if I start on the 27th of October, I read the 27th Proverb. That is how to do a book-by-book, verse-by-verse study. You will be amazed at what you will learn and surprised to discover the number of things you've been wrong about.

The Bible is not complicated. That is Satan's lie. Many people stay away from the book of Revelations because they believe it is too hard, but I learned in Florida Bible College to read the verse before and the verse after. Also, once you have accepted Christ as your Savior you have the Holy Spirit inside of you. Do you know what the Holy Spirit's job is? In John 16:8 (KJV), Jesus says, "When the Holy Spirit comes, He will convict the world of sin, righteousness, and judgment." In John 14:16 (KJV), Jesus states, "And I will pray the Father, and he shall give you another Comforter, that he may abide with you for ever." In other words, no one in this world can come to Christ without the Holy Spirit convicting them that they are a sinner and convincing them of their need for a Savior.

When it comes to reading the Bible, one other aspect of the Holy Spirit is found in John 14:26(ESV), where Jesus told his disciples, "But the Helper, the Holy Spirit, whom the Father will send in my name, he will teach you all things and bring to your remembrance all that I have said to you." What a wonderful thing it is for us to know that when we accept Christ, we receive the Holy Spirit. One of His jobs is to teach us and help bring to memory the things we have learned, which is why it is so important to read and study God's word. You cannot recall to memory the things you have not learned. It is impossible.

Often, when I share the gospel with someone, the Holy Spirit brings to mind a passage. When I communicate the passage to an individual, they will sometimes share that they were thinking about the very issue the passage addresses. Our God is an absolutely amazing God. We never have to be ashamed of Him or His Word. When we stand on God's foundation— His Word, we are indeed on solid ground.

Here is another significant fact about studying the Word of God. Many of us have ideas and behaviors that are contrary to the Bible. Some of these are unconscious patterns we develop in childhood and may not even be aware of having. As we study the Word, God starts changing our thoughts and behavior patterns. Sometimes, we might not initially recognize the changes.

We must use the Bible as our plumb line to examine ourselves the way the Lord wants us to. If we do not, we are influenced by social media and those around us. Often, those influences are contrary to the Word. When I work with married couples, I tell them marriage is like a golf game. If, when golfing, you change one thing about your swing, you will end up changing everything about your game. Many couples come to me with countless issues, feeling that their marriage is hopeless. But, if they can hone in on one thing and work on it, they will begin to see change.

It takes about six weeks to develop a new habit, so couples have to be patient and commit to several weeks of regular counseling. A 40-year-old marriage can't be fixed in 3 weeks. I cannot stress enough the importance of also spending devotional time together. Even 15 minutes of daily reading and praying together draws couples closer to the Lord and each other. Ruth Graham (Billy Graham's wife) once said that besides the Bible, *My Upmost For His Highest* was her favorite devotional. I recommend you give it a read.

You will never be a perfect Christian until the Lord brings you home. Ask the Lord to show you something you must work on to be more Christ-like, and He will. As you work on one thing, the Lord will show you something else and on and on it goes until you no longer wish to grow in your Christian life or you go home to be with the Lord. People have asked me, "When will I stop growing in my Christian life? The answer is, "As long as we conform our minds to the scripture instead of holding by our traditions, we will keep growing in our faith." This is known as exegesis, an objective method of interpreting a text. On the other hand, eisegesis is a subjective method that involves imposing our own ideas on the text that we were previously taught. For example, most people believe that the fruit that Adam ate was an apple. However, the Bible never says what it is. Maybe it was a banana because it had appeal. Get it?

Do you ever wonder why God's Word is called the growing word of God? It is because you never stop learning about God's truths. He will take you through a passage, and then the next time you read it, He will take you to a deeper level. Each time you read, you will learn something new; that's why it's so important to keep reading and learning. I had a dear pastor who called this TAG—time alone with God every day. Let's TAG along with Jesus and see what He will teach you.

What does examining yourself look like? Galatians 5:22–23(KJV) says, "But the fruit of the Spirit is love, joy, peace, longsuffering, gentleness, goodness, faith, Meekness, temperance against such there is no law." So, how much of us does the Holy Spirit possess? Do you have hatred in your heart toward someone? Do your actions convey your joy?

Is your joy enough to make people wonder why you appear so happy? Remember, joy is different than happiness, as we discussed earlier. Do you have peace in the midst of a storm? Do you have confidence in Jesus to work things out for good (Romans 8:28) even when things seem bleak? Does it take you a long time to get upset, or are you a ticking time bomb? Are you a person who shows kindness and gentleness to others and displays an unshakable faith? These things may seem impossible when you are apart from the Holy Spirit, who gives us the power to display Christ in us.

As Christians, we receive all of the Holy Spirit as soon as we are saved. "But you are not controlled by your sinful nature. You are controlled by the Spirit if you have the Spirit of God living in you. (And remember that those who do not have the Spirit of Christ living in them do not belong to him at all.)" (Romans 8:9, NLT). Notice the word controlled. We get 100% of the Holy Spirit when we trust Christ. However, how much control He has over us fluctuates on a daily basis.

How often do we think *I feel really close to the Lord today, or I think I handled that in a way that was pleasing to the Lord.* Then, the next day or situation is a different story. Just as a baby doesn't start walking without falling, we must exercise our new nature in Christ every day by being in the Word and walking close to Him.

Let's consider addiction. There are some Christians who believe a *real* Christian cannot be addicted to drugs, alcohol, sex, or a number of other addictions. This is entirely false. Some people get saved and instantly stop being addicts, but unfortunately, that is not often the case. I believe the Christian approach to helping those who are addicted should not be the same as the world. After all, we have the spirit of Christ in us, and He wants us to be victorious.

Matthew 11:28–30 (ESV) states, "Come to me, all you who labor and are heavy laden, and I will give you rest. Take my yoke upon you and learn from me, for I am gentle and lowly in heart, and you will find rest for your souls. For my yoke is easy and my burden is light." What does it mean to take the Lord's yoke? It is to humbly do His will and allow Him to guide and direct our lives. In other words, don't focus on your addiction. Focus on letting the Lord take the addiction and diving into the Word. Start doing things that you enjoy and are pleasing to Him. Open your life and have fellowship. Join a group of believers who know and teach the word. Often, programs will teach people how to manage their addiction, but the Lord tells us we are overcomers, not managers!

> "These things I have spoken to you so that in Me you may have peace. In the world you have tribulation, but take courage; I have overcome the world."
>
> —John 16:33, (NASB)

> "And Jesus answered and said to them, "Truly I say to you, if you have faith and do not doubt, you will not only do what was done to the fig tree, but even if you say to this mountain, 'Be taken up and cast into the sea,' it will happen."
>
> —Matthew 21:21 (NASB)

I have learned by examining my life that I can't vindicate myself for the road the Lord has taken me down. One thing I have gleaned from reading *My Upmost For His Highest* is how Christ often takes us down a path. Oswald Chambers explains, "God doesn't call us to common things but to display the character of God." What is the character of God? *Love, joy, peace, longsuffering,* and up close and personal *forgiveness.* Sometimes, God calls someone to a life that other people consider crazy. I'm sure many missionaries and pastors have heard, "You are throwing your life away; how will you provide for your family?" And the list goes on and on.

How many people have capitulated and decided not to take the route the Lord is showing them because of pressure from family and friends? How do you know what is really God's will? We do what His Word tells us.

1. Spend time in prayer with the Lord.
2. Read God's word, verse-by-verse and book-by-book, daily.
3. Have fellowship with believers.
4. Every Christian receives a spiritual gift when they accept Christ as their Savior. Exercise your gift by using it for the body of Christ.
5. Witness to family, friends, and the people the Lord puts in your path: neighbors, delivery people, salespeople,

etc. As I said before, I love the ministry of *Moments With The Book.* They produce all kinds of tracts that help you get a conversation started with strangers. A good practice is to begin by saying, "I'd like to give you this. It tells you how much God loves you and cares for you."

If you are doing the items listed above, the Lord will show you His will. As Henry Blackaby says in his incredible book *Experiencing God,* "God is always at work around us." God isn't trying to hide His will and keep it from us. Just as a good parent guides a child, He wants to guide us into His truth and show us His will so we will walk in it. Psalms 86:11 (NIV) is a great verse for us to pray. "Teach me your way, LORD, that I may rely on your faithfulness; give me an undivided heart, that I may fear your name."

Many Christians are constantly asking the Lord to show them His will but don't do the things God tells them to do. God reveals His will in many different ways: through His Word, television programs, news outlets, people, circumstances, and small opportunities that lead to bigger challenges. He is surely at work all around us.

Let me give you an example. I worked in an emergency room as a liaison between staff and patients. There was a girl who transported patients from their rooms to surgery, and anywhere else they were assigned to go. Pushing stretchers and wheel-chairs all day is a difficult job. One day, she came to me in tears and said she wanted to quit. She couldn't stand her job any longer. I talked to her and said, "You are single, and quitting will lead to hardship. You don't know how long it will be before another opportunity comes along. Think about this: while you are trans-porting the patients, you have their full attention. They don't have family, friends, a cell phone, or any other distractions. Use the time to engage with them. Most people have some anxiety about going into surgery, so talk to them and show an interest in the subjects they wish to discuss. You never know how your kindness could lead to another open door." Guess what? Two weeks later she came to me all smiles. She told me, "I did what you said, and you were right." After I began a conversation with one of the patients, he said to me, "I own a car dealership, and I am looking for a person to head up the office. I need someone who can deal with all types of people, and I would like you to come in for an interview." She got the job and started two weeks later. Nothing had changed about her job, just her attitude. She let people see her concern for them, and the Lord used this to open a door for her.

I love the song *Sometimes He Calms The Storm* by Scott Krippayne. We often pray to God and ask him to take away or change the circumstances we find ourselves in, but the Lord frequently wants us to rest and find peace in Him during our challenges. Work, marriage, children, parents, family, and friends will all be difficult at times. Instead of asking the Lord to change *them*, ask Him to change *you* and love them through you.

When you strongly feel the Lord is leading you down a particular road, try not to take it personally if people say you are crazy or that you must be mistaken. Be aware that a lot of people do not seek God's face before they decide to criticize you. Stand fast. It will not be easy, and they may never come around or accept God's will for you. Delight in the knowledge that you are walking the steps the Lord wants you to walk. He is omniscient. He knows you love Him and are trying to follow His ways. I love what Galatians 6:9 (KJV) says, "And let us not be weary in well doing:

for in due season we shall reap, if we faint not." Notice the phrase *in due season;* it does not mean right away, a year, five, or even ten years from now. So be faithful, and although the results you desire may not come about, you will be blessed when you put yourself in God's hands.

It is easy for us to become Christians. It was hard for God. He sent His only son. But it is not easy for us to become Christ-like. Being Christ-like takes the strength and determination to fight against our flesh, which wants the pleasures and benefits of this life. Consider this: Anybody who has broken their arm or leg knows how weak it is when the cast is finally taken off. It's hard to lift your arm or walk. Now imagine babying it and refusing to use it. It would eventually atrophy and become useless.

When we become Christians, we have the Holy Spirit inside of us. However, we need to learn to give Him more and more control every day by denying our flesh. Our flesh is strong because we have nourished and fed it all the years we have been unsaved. Every time we give into pleasure, we go against God's will. Having sex outside of marriage, pride, getting upset when things don't go our way, unkindness, and giving into addiction are examples of feeding the flesh and making it stronger.

When we do the things that are pleasing to the Lord, we make our new nature stronger to resist Satan and our flesh, which are constantly tempting us. *The Screwtape Letters* by C.S. Lewis is a masterpiece that helps us understand how much Satan tries to trap us into destroying our lives. Screwtape is a devil who teaches his nephew, Wormwood, how to convince his assigned human, *The Patient*, to reject Christ. However, Wormwood fails, and The Patient turns to the Lord, leaving Wormwood with the task of devising ways to destroy The Patient's life.

Satan is the reason we see so many people doing crazy things in the news and all around us. It is Satan that prevents people from seeing the consequences of their behavior. Many people who are caught in the aftermath of a grievous sin will think to themselves; *I can't believe I did that. I never thought of all the grief this would bring to myself and others.* If you are struggling with a deep sin, below are some steps to consider:

- Confession is difficult, but it is better

than being *found out*. Talk with a good Christian counselor or attorney. Do not keep burying your feelings. Being secretive and avoiding others will just compound the problem. Psalm 19:12–14 (GNT), "None of us can see our own errors; deliver me, LORD from hidden faults! Keep me safe, also, from willful sins; don't let them rule over me. Then I shall be perfect and free from the evil of sin. May my words and my thoughts be acceptable to you, O LORD, my refuge and my redeemer!"

- Know that the depth of deception will increase as time goes by. Don't think you can keep sin in a little corner of your life. It will spread to other areas. Anger and bitterness will grow like a tree, and you will start acting it out to get back at the person. Sin is like yeast in dough. It doesn't take long before it spreads to the whole loaf. (Galatians 5:9).

- Sin in your life affects those around you. Your flesh may say: it's not a big deal, I can stop at any time, I'm not hurting anyone, this is just something that temporarily suits my needs, or I will deal with the sin later. But Satan is setting you up for a moral failure whose tentacles will reach far and wide. A long time ago, I heard a saying that I have never forgotten. "Sin will take you further than you wanted to go, keep you longer than you wanted to stay, and cost you more than you wanted to pay."

- Don't forget you are not alone. One of the most powerful verses on temptation is I Corinthians 10:13 (ESV), "God is faithful, and he will not let you be tempted beyond your ability, but with the temptation he will also provide the way of escape, that you may be able to endure it." Notice it says God is Faithful, not that we are faithful. Call on God in repentance and ask Him for deliverance, and then be willing to do the work. Crying out to the Lord and telling Him how you feel is getting close to Him. He knows our faults, but it strengthens the closeness of the relationship when we confess to Him.

- Return to the things that you once enjoyed. Invariably people will stop doing the things they enjoyed when they are feeding the sin in their lives. We are all busy people, and in America, we are part of a culture that prides itself on being busy. Take a few minutes to unwind before starting another task. Enjoy the day, read a few pages of a book, or call a friend (catching up can be done while you're doing the dishes or taking a walk). I had four children, all two years apart, and I assure you it's impossible to take care of others well if you don't take care of yourself.

- Be aware of those around you. Everybody knows it is hard to go against the tide. If your friends are serving the Lord and doing His will, it will be much easier to learn from them and do the same. On the flip side, if your friends think it's crazy to do all the *religious stuff* you will need new friends, ones that are delighted with the Lord. That is the reason God tells us to assemble with other believers, so we can encourage and be encouraged by them. (Hebrews 10:25).

- Most of all pray. As we discussed in I Corinthians 10:13, God is faithful, and He will not allow you to be tempted beyond what you can bear. Plead with the Lord to guide you and provide a way out. He will always provide a way if we ask Him to. Sin is a substitute for the gifts God wants to give us. If we are looking for a way to escape, someone who desires or loves us, or if we have a need to feel valued, God can and will provide it. However, we must seek Him through prayer, fellowship, and by reading His Word. He will fill up the empty places in our lives if we ask and follow Him.

By putting these steps into your life, you will begin to enjoy peace and joy like you have never known. Being freed from the bondage of sin and its effects is a life that unbelievers do not know. Only people who have given their life to Christ and have the Holy Spirit in their lives understand the joy of a life with Christ.

Let me give you this word picture. Suppose you are the daughter of the most powerful person on earth. Would you have money troubles? No. Your Dad would take care of you. What about when you have relationship issues? You would talk to your Dad. Do you see where I am going with this? Once you trust Christ, you are a child of the King. You are a prince or a princess. But as with your earthly father and mother, you still have to do the work of building the relationship. God says in Ephesians 2:10 (ESV), "For we are his workmanship created in Christ Jesus for good works, which God prepared beforehand that we should walk in them."

God has a multitude of good things for us to do. The problem is we get in the way. We are selfish and want things our way, and that sidetracks our lives. I love Garth Brook's song *Unanswered Prayers,* even though I'm not a country music fan. I'm a Jersey girl, but *Unanswered Prayers* has a deep meaning. In it, he prays to be with his high school sweetheart forever.

Later in life, he is with his wife, and he runs into his high school sweetheart. Immediately he realizes she does not compare to his wife, so he thanks God for unanswered prayers. God wants to orchestrate our lives and make it beautiful. He just needs us to ask and be willing to let go so He can take us, down the road, toward what He wants us to do and become.

10
ANXIETY AND FEARS

Two of Satan's greatest tools are hang-ups and fears. Hang-ups and fears hold many people, who don't even realize it, prisoners. They keep you from achieving God's best, and prevent you from obeying and believing God's Word because what God wants you to do doesn't always appear to make sense.

II Timothy 1:7 (KJV) explains, "For God hath not given us the spirit of fear; but of power, and of love, and of sound mind." However, if you have the spirit of fear, the opposite occurs, and you do not have a sound mind. Fear manifests itself in many ways. There are rational fears (like a fear of fire) that God gives us to keep us safe. Then, there are irrational fears that often come from what we hear or believe. These fears are not Biblical.

Watching the news too much and neglecting the Word of God can create enormous amounts of fear. Many people are afraid of getting hurt, so they refuse to reconcile with someone who has genuinely shown repentance. They claim forgiveness but want nothing to do with the person. How do you let this person back into your life? Here are some steps to take:

Make sure there is genuine repentance and that they aren't sorry simply because they were caught but genuinely want to make amends to the person they have hurt. How will you know? Take the time to examine their life. Ask the Lord in prayer to show you the truth. I am confident that when you honestly seek God, He will show Himself. Many Christians raised in faith still do not believe in Christ's complete payment for sin. They grow up feeling deceived and then want nothing to do with any faith. Yet if they honestly give God a chance and seek the truth, the Lord will show it. Instead, they settle for a substitute and reject God's greatest gift of salvation: His son. Most importantly, The world does not believe a person can change. Real change is a heart change. II Corinthians 5:17 (NKJV) says, "Therefore, if anyone is in Christ, *he is* a new creation; old things have passed away; behold, all things have become new." Accepting Christ and taking His Word over your feelings changes the way you think and behave.

I caution churches to examine faith-based programs that help people *cope* with addiction. Christ did not send His Son to help us cope with sin but to conquer and free us completely from the wage of sin, which is death (Romans 6:23). If His payment can keep us out of hell, don't you think He is powerful enough to help you overcome your sin or addiction? I am not claiming we can get to a point where we no longer sin. We will always have a sinful nature until we die and go to glory. However, as you rely more deeply on Christ and build up your Christian work, you will achieve victory from the sin you are currently battling. Then, the Lord will show you something new to work on so you can become more Christ-like.

I have evaluated AA programs prior to referring my clients. At one of my evaluations, I heard an engaging speaker. He said that when you have addictions, it covers up feelings a person would typically experience. He further explained. He had started drinking when he was a teenager and continued into his 30s. After 25 years of sobriety, he remained a committed member of the AA program. He recalled an instance when, after first getting sober, he met a woman and desperately wanted to ask her out. But he felt terrified. He talked about his hands sweating and his heart racing. Confused, he wondered at his fear. However, he soon realized that in all the years he spent drinking, he had been covering the feelings that most adolescents go through. He had not felt those emotions, and it was time to *face the music*. In other words, you stop emotionally in several areas of life when you use a substance to avoid dealing with issues or pain.

Stuffing emotions doesn't only happen with substance abuse. Good things like running, exercising, watching T.V., and hobbies can also be used. If you use anything to avoid dealing with your pain, it will be detrimental. Opening up and dealing with life's hurts, regardless of how deep they may be, will free you and those around you. If you have a particular lifestyle or habit that is excessive, look at why and examine your motives.

I read the book *Into Thin Air*. It is about a Mount Everest climbing disaster that resulted in the death of eight climbers. The author describes his obsession with his hobby and how it almost resulted in the loss of his family due to the time and money he spent on it. Are you doing something to deaden your pain? Are you thinking you are better off not dealing with it? You are not, and it will eventually damage your life if you let it.

We are to become overcomers, not just managers. No matter how much you feel you are in bondage, the Lord wants to break your chains and help you experience the love and joy you can have in Christ. I never want my clients who have gained victory over addiction to continue to call themselves alcoholics or drug users. I tell them God heals completely, not halfway, but it is a battle that you must join Him in to win.

Don't ever believe the sin you have committed is a way of life and you will never gain deliverance. It is not! That is the world's thinking. When you give your addiction to Jesus Christ and seek Him, God promises: "So if the Son sets you free, you will be free indeed." John 8:36, (NIV). Christians who have never had an addiction need to stop believing what the world says. *He'll go back to being an addict as soon as he gets a chance; he has had an addiction his whole life and will die that way. These people never change, and I would never do that.* Maybe you would never do what they have done, but you'll fall in some other way. Don't think that others are somehow less worthy. You never know the circumstances they have faced. Remember,

"There by the grace of God go I."

Please stop thinking; *He did that even though he was supposedly saved, so he must not have been truly saved at the time.* First of all, once you come to Christ, you have a new nature. However, you still have your old nature, and it continues to fight for dominance. The only way you can strengthen your new nature is by giving more of your life to Christ. As I've said before, you do this by reading the Word, praying, fellowshipping with other believers, telling others about Christ's way of salvation, and using your gifts for the Lord.

Remember, God does not forgive the unsaved more than the saved. You are a child of God, and He loves you beyond human comprehension. Christians have committed all the same sins the unsaved have committed. However, as a child of God, you can be totally restored, not managing sin but totally freed. You can experience a new life in Christ by the way of repentance.

Christ was the most rejected man on earth. He was also the most perfect man that ever walked the earth. People will question your faith and sanity if you walk on the path that the Lord has led you on. The road that leads to the ways of Christ is narrow (Matthew 7:13). Will you allow God to take you by the hand, conquer your fears, and lead you to a life of fearlessness?

John 10:10 (KJV) exclaims, "The thief cometh not, but for to steal, and to kill, and to destroy: I am come that they might have life, and that they might have it more abundantly." God doesn't want you to live your life by putting one foot in front of the other every day and just surviving. He wants you to **THRIVE!** What is keeping you from thriving? Don't give in to your fears and anxieties; doing so will only exacerbate them.

Imagine that someone has been bitten by a dog when they were young. They then avoid all dogs and do not want to be around them. They have transported their fear into believing *all dogs are dangerous and they must not ever be around them.*

Then, low and behold, they meet someone who is a dog lover. What can they do? They can stay away from the person, or they can gradually assuage their fear and get to know the dog. Soon, they may realize that not all dogs are waiting for an opportunity to attack.

I use this example because I have experienced this. When I first met my husband, he didn't have any experience with owning a house pet. He had been a newspaper boy and had grown to dislike dogs because they would bark and chase him.

I, on the other hand, am an animal lover. I love to go up to people and see their eyes light up when I want to pet their dog. I had a beagle and a lab mix named Jersey. I'm from New Jersey, so as you can see, I'm very original. When we discussed marriage, I told him, "Jersey is not going to be an outside dog. I don't believe in that. Either the animal is a pet, or we don't have them." He said, "Well, Jersey is a good dog." We got married, and he was nice to Jersey, but he kept his distance. He wasn't overly affectionate. I used to tell Jersey, "Now you have to realize that you are an ambassador for all dogs. Your job is to help Daddy see how nice dogs are."

In time, because he was around her, he started warming up to Jersey. So much so that when I went to Tennessee to visit my daughter, he took Jersey to work with him since he worked at a place that encouraged the workers to bring their dogs. So, what did he gain from this change? He gained a great marriage, a godly partner in life, and an ability to befriend people with dogs without fear or anxiety.

Giving in to fears can have far-reaching consequences, not only for you but for friends and family. I have a book in my office called *Kids Who Carry Your Pain.* It is about children who have grown up with their parent's fears and anxieties and now carry the same. To them, it is normal.

My mother was terrified of drowning. She was in the water when she was young and felt that she was drowning. Because of that, I could have easily stayed away from swimming. However, I learned to swim and loved the water. I was even on the swim team when I was in high school. My mom, to her credit, used to take my brother and me to the lake after school, which I loved. My children learned to swim when they were very young, and I am grateful that I was not afraid of letting them play in the water. It's easy to see how fear can spread if we let it.

Remember, as we read before in II Timothy

1:7 (KJV), God has not given us the spirit of fear but of power, love, and a sound mind. There is something else to consider: if God has not given you the spirit of fear, who has? Satan loves to create fearfulness since it is the opposite of trust. Jesus specifically mentions one fear in the Bible: *the fear of death*. Fear of death is the driving force for many these days. People strive to look younger by getting plastic surgery, which is a booming business, and purchasing all types of age-fighting products and makeup. The fitness industry can also attest to this. It is great to be healthy and fit, but the excessive drive to fight against death and aging is a futile endeavor.

I Corinthians 15:55–57 (NIV) proclaims, "'Where, O death, is your victory? Where, O death, is your sting?' The sting of death is sin, and the power of sin is the law. But thanks be to God! He gives us the victory through our Lord Jesus Christ.'" Unless Jesus comes back in our lifetime, and I believe He will, we all will experience death. Jesus promises to take the sting or fear of death from those who know Him—trusting Christ as Savior is not just a golden ticket to heaven. It affects your whole life when you know you are in His hands and when dead will be going to heaven.

You do not stop living life. On the contrary, you live life to the fullest, knowing what is done for Christ will last (II Corinthians 4:18). How is this possible, you may ask? God is a scorekeeper. He knows every thought, every kindness, harsh word, lie, and deed you have ever done, but knowing this does not have to be a scary thought. As we discussed in Galatians 6:7–9, reaping what you sow is great when you are sowing good seeds. You might be wondering about all your past sins. They are not only forgiven, but God will not bring them up again. However, the unbelievers will have their sins brought forward at the great white throne of judgment. By confessing our sins, we help create a relationship bond with Christ. Let's say a friend is hurtful towards you. You discuss it with them and they don't admit their wrongdoing. Forgive them anyway, and don't bring it up again. Doing so will help to establish the relationship. However, the bond would be stronger if they admit to hurting you.

Pride is the biggest barrier to having a short list with Jesus. By that, I mean when we pray, Jesus will bring situations to our minds. It may be something we haven't dealt with or someone we have possibly hurt. Deal with it in a timely manner so you can continue to allow the Holy Spirit's work in your life and not quench Him (I Thessalonians 5:19.) Sometimes, people don't want to confess because they are afraid they may do it again.

Do parents say, "Why are you telling me this? You're just going to do it again," when a child says sorry? No. Parents want to teach their children, so they explain the reasons why their actions are wrong. If a child lies, parents could admonish them for lying, or they could teach them about the little boy who cried wolf and discuss how they should be a person of their word. The latter is preferable since it is a principle the child can apply to many situations. This is how God is with us. He wants us to learn from our mistakes and to see the grace that He gives us every day. The Lord never tires of us asking for forgiveness or praying for help. He loves us more than words can say.

How do you incorporate these Biblical principles into your life? First, and most importantly, develop a prayer life. Jesus, who knew His time was short on earth and who had the most critical ministry in the world, took time out to turn to the Father in prayer. In scriptures there are many times Jesus stopped to pray. Should we do less? An excellent guide is to pray *ACTS*.

A–Acknowledge:

Acknowledge God for who He is. There are many names for God, and I thank Him for these every day: Jehovah, Jireh—the Lord, my provider. He provides my needs, and also my wants when they are in His will. Jehovah Rapha—the God who gives me health. Not only does He provide me with health but also vitality. I believe He has blessed me for taking care of myself, but I also acknowledge that there are plenty of people who struggle with health issues through no fault of their own. However, I do believe we have to accept our part in our health. Abusing our body and then asking God for health is doing what we want to do but not expecting God to give us consequences. Jehovah Nissi—the Lord our banner, He has the victory in our lives if we submit to His will and let Him have free reign in our lives.

Then I thank God for His omniscience—all-knowing, omnipresence—He is everywhere, and omnipotence—all-powerful. When we try to do God's will, we can be at rest with the knowledge that He sees us. He knows our motives and thoughts. He promises to be strong on behalf of those whose hearts are perfect toward Him. I love the way II Chronicles

16:9 (NKJV) puts it, "For the eyes of the LORD run to and fro throughout the whole earth, to show Himself strong on behalf of *those* whose heart *is* loyal toward Him." That does not mean that God expects us to be perfect in character but perfect in commitment.

C–Confession:

As we said earlier, keep a short list with God. Remember when you sinned and felt guilty but made no confession? What happened? It became easier the next time. People fall into a slippery slope when they feel guilt but ignore it. They become harder and harder as time goes on. I Timothy 4:2 talks about people who have their conscience seared with a hot iron. Once you have seared a piece of material with a hot iron, it is hard to separate it. That's why we are often amazed when Christians commit a deep sin. It always starts with them ignoring the conviction of the Holy Spirit, and then the sin continues until it gets easier and easier. Eventually, they lose their feelings of guilt. When I counsel, I talk about good guilt and bad guilt. Bad guilt is when you have been convicted of sin, have repented, and yet refuse to accept God's forgiveness. It is when you continue living your life like a second-class citizen. Good guilt is when you have sinned; your guilt has driven you to confess, turn away from the sin, and start doing positive things for the Lord.

Remember, when we talk about confessing our sins, we are not talking about avoiding the consequences of sin. There are ramifications, but God can still allow you to thrive. How many people are born into this world through unmarried parents? Many of these children not only become a blessing in their own right but also bring their parents to Christ.

Even if you are thinking: You don't know what I have done. My life is useless. It's over. I encourage you to repent, give your life to Christ, try to make amends where you can, and be determined to ignore those who feel you have nothing to offer. Don't waste your time trying to vindicate yourself to people who refuse to accept your repentance. There are many Christians who think the same way the world does —*he will never change, he is a threat to my family, or I don't want anything to do with him.* You can waste a lot of time trying to convince these people of your repentance. Live your life for Christ, and let those who genuinely want to live by godly principles see your life.

T–Thanksgiving:

Someone once said to me, "How many things would you have tomorrow if God took away all the things that you never thanked him for today?" I have never forgotten it. It is quite thought-provoking. We are always ready to ask God for things, but how about thanking Him for all the blessings we already have!

S–Supplication:

Supplication is asking God to bless us and find favor with us. When we follow the Lord, He wants to use us in a mighty way. Carry a little notebook with you and write down people's names and requests so you don't forget. I have a few pages of people that I pray for every day. I pray for my family by name, friends, and many who do not know Christ as their Savior. There are also requests which I number 1–7. I pray for all the ones on Sundays, the twos on Mondays, and so on. It is a good system because I would forget people if I didn't write them down. Finally, I mark in black and white the answered requests along with the date. Sometimes, when I look back and see unanswered requests, I feel glad that the Lord said no since He knows what is best.

I used to listen to a program out of Canada that talked about *God Spy*. *God Spy* refers to the things God does all around us. Sometimes, if we are not paying attention, we don't notice them. Angels are guarding us (Hebrews 1:14). And with God before us, who can be against us? (Romans 8:31). God still moves mountains. There are many Scriptural examples of God doing things man would call impossible. Daniel was unharmed in the lion's den. David killed the giant Goliath with only one stone and a sling. Joseph, a Jewish man, became second to Pharaoh in Egypt, and Paul, a pharisee, radically changed when he accepted Jesus as the true Messiah.

We may think our circumstances are impossible, but "For with God nothing shall be impossible." Luke 1:37 (KJV). And Philippians 4:13 (NKJV) says, "I can do all things through Christ who strengthens me." We often miss *God Spy* because we get caught up with the world's thinking—*That was lucky, what a coincidence, and you were in the right place at the right time.* Even Christians forget that God orchestrates our lives and works things out for our good. Romans 8:28 (NIV) is a valuable verse to keep in mind, "And we know that in all things God works for the good of those who love him, who have been called according to his purpose."

As you grow in your faith, you will gradually learn to listen to God's voice, not audibly, for the most part, but God is working on us to be like Him throughout our entire lives. I believe people sometimes fight against giving up control when they know about God orchestrating their lives, especially if they don't have good relationships with their fathers or other family members and have trust issues. The Lord wants the best for you, but that doesn't mean every day will be filled with bliss and you will walk on roses.

Christians are not perfect—just forgiven. Do you think I display these principles all the time? Think again. I am a sinner saved by grace—no more and no less. The flesh always desires to do the opposite of what the Lord wants us to do, and it is easier to follow the flesh, but it is a daily necessity to walk in the ways of the Lord, even when it is not our natural path.

We want to treat people the way they treat

us—if they are nasty, we want to reciprocate or, at best, completely ignore them. It is easier to hold a grudge and remove those who have sinned against us from our lives than to forgive them. We may think we are justified, but how about extending the hand of friendship and walking alongside the sinner on his journey to recovery? As John F. Kennedy quoted Edmund Burke in 1961, "The only thing necessary to the triumph of evil is for good men to do nothing."

Using these principles to heal your life:

Now that you are familiar with these biblical principles, how do you use them for healing? *Application.* In my practice, I see many people who love the Lord and read the Word but are struggling with addiction, anxiety, self-worth, self-control, depression, or some other malady that the world has to offer. These are some of the reasons that we do not see more people living the abundant life that the Bible talks about. (John 10:10)

We are meant to be the light of the world. Matthew 5:16 (KJV) says, "Let your light so shine before men, that they may see your good works, and glorify your Father which is in heaven." As the world is getting darker, our light should shine brighter. When we are in a totally dark room, we are instantly attracted to a lit candle. Our lives should be so attractive to the world around us that we are seen as different, in a good way, and others will want to know the reason for our joy. A good example of what I mean occurred when I lived in New Jersey. Several of us were working and sprucing things up at our church. We were joking, laughing and enjoying ourselves while we worked. A neighbor came over and said he noticed how we seemed to really enjoy each other, and he wanted to know what the church was about. What a witnessing opportunity we had that day! When I say let your light shine, that is the type of thing I am talking about.

Inner joy comes from knowing Jesus healed you from your hang-ups and is in your corner. He is an advocate for you before God Himself. I John 2:1 (NIV) reads, "My dear children, I write this to you so that you will not sin. But if anybody does sin, we have an advocate with the Father–Jesus Christ, the Righteous One." We all have sin, but there is grace and mercy; when we repent, there is restoration and fellowship with Christ.

James is a powerful passage on temptation. Falling into deep sin will give consequences you might have never considered. Satan is like a roaring lion prowling about seeking whom he may devour (I Peter 5:8). Satan has been looking for men to destroy since Adam and Eve. He is very good at it by now. I don't feel that enough Christians fear God and Satan. They work at church, spend hours on their jobs, join sports, or participate in several other activities, and they don't choose to read the Word of God and build a relationship with Him.

How do you build a relationship with God? How do you build a relationship with your friends? You spend time with them, and you share your thoughts and dreams. You want to make them happy by knowing what makes them happy—these are all the things the Lord wants for us. What do you reap in return? You reap the power to overcome temptation, our anxieties, our depression, and our addictions.

One of the greatest tools our flesh has is isolation. You are not alone in this battle. James 1:13–15 (KJV) describes how Satan works: "Let no man say when he is tempted; I am tempted of God: for God cannot be tempted with evil, neither tempteth he any man: But every man is tempted, when he is drawn away of his own lust, and enticed. Then when lust hath conceived, it brings forth sin: and sin, when it is finished, brings forth death." Notice that it is not a sin to be tempted; it is common to all men. However, when it is acted upon, it brings sin, and sin brings forth death.

Does that mean if you act on temptation, God will strike you dead? Probably not. But it is a spiritual death, not a loss of salvation but a loss of fellowship with Christ, a loss of reputation, and you may never get it back. There could be more consequences than you have ever imagined. When you are in a spiritual battle, God promises that if you call on him, He will make a way to escape. Commit this verse to *memory.* I Corinthians 10:13 (KJV), "There hath no temptation taken you but such as is common to man: but God is faithful, who will not suffer you to be tempted above that ye are able; but will with the temptation also make a way to escape, that ye may be able to bear it."

What do I mean when I say *Get Out?* If you are tempted at work, *Leave.* I know this may sound impossible for some of you, but many people start flirtations at work that lead to disaster and would do anything to take it back. The Lord will take care of you if you commit to doing the right thing. You might have to switch jobs or locations. The crucial point is to *leave*. Never start confiding in a person of the opposite sex if you are married! This can lead to the development of a friendship with that person instead of closeness with your spouse. You may be thinking there is no way you can leave your job. But, believe me, Satan will use your hesitation to dig you deeper and deeper into sin. Remember what I said earlier: with repentance, there is restoration of the relationship between the Lord and you. However, giving in to temptation can lead to the destruction of your family and cause you to hurt them.

Sin is pleasurable. Hebrews 11:24–26 (KJV), the faith chapter in the Bible, talks about Moses' refusal to give into temptation. "By faith Moses, when he was come to years, refused to be called the son of Pharaoh's daughter; Choosing rather to suffer affliction with the people of God, than to enjoy the pleasures of sin for a season; Esteeming the reproach of Christ greater riches than the treasures in Egypt: for he had respect for the recompense of the reward."

Exodus 2 is a fantastic story on temptation. Moses was called the son of Pharaoh's daughter even though, by birth, he was the son of enslaved Jews. Pharaoh wanted to destroy all the Jewish babies because the Jewish people outnumbered the Egyptians. Therefore, Moses' mother hid him in a basket and released it into the Nile. The floating basket was found and brought to Pharaoh's daughter. When Moses grew, he discovered his Jewish heritage, and rather than remaining in Pharaoh's luxury he chose to leave and suffer the affliction with his people.

Moses did many great deeds, including leading the children of Israel out of Egypt, but we forget that he had to take the first step by denying himself all the pleasures and riches that Egypt had to offer. He then lived in the desert for 40 years before hearing from God. We must be like Moses and take the first step by denying ourselves what is pleasurable to us and giving the Lord the chance to bless our decisions. God is faithful.

We look at what tempts us and think, *This is what I need. This will fill the empty space in my life.* But temptation is a poor substitute that can lead to the total destruction of the life you currently know. There is always hope. There is always a way out. Take the first step, and don't worry about what will happen two or three years down the road. Do what God is asking you to do and *escape* your way to happiness and joy down the road.

You will be tempted to turn back. You will question whether you did the right thing by not giving in. Use that time to have fellowship with other believers. Get in God's Word, and develop a relationship with a fellow Christian or counselor who will help you through the difficult times. Confess to the Lord and move forward. I have had clients tell me, "I never believed I could be this happy." Believe it. God will never ask anything of you that He will not give you the power to do. But like a light, you have to be plugged in. When you plug into our Lord Jesus Christ, you become a light source for others and a living, breathing example of the joy that Christ can bring.

Knowing and incorporating the principles from this book will help you with your interpersonal relationships, especially with those closest to you, your family and friends. When you become a complete person, your reactions to those around you will change. For example, if a mom has doubts about herself, lacks self-confidence, and doesn't know who she is in Christ, she will look for validation from her children. She will need them to behave and do well so she can feel good about herself. Instead of seeing some of their antics as those of typical kid, she will see their disobedience as a vendetta against her. So, allowing the Lord to transform her also changes the lives of those affected by her behavior.

An incredibly powerful scriptural passage and one that every Christian should know is Romans 12:19–21 (NIV), which reads, "Do not take revenge, my dear friends, but leave room for God's wrath, for it is written: 'It is mine to avenge; I will repay,' says the Lord. On the contrary: If your enemy is hungry, feed him; if he is thirsty, give him something to drink. In doing this, you will heap burning coals on his head. Do not be overcome by evil, but overcome evil with good."

If we believe what Romans 12:19–21 says, then we will be freed from thinking we have to vindicate ourselves or seek revenge. However, a lot of people don't think about God's attribute of retribution, and punishment, which is often overlooked in the teachings. It is just as powerful as God's love and forgiveness. Knowing when we are wronged and treated unjustly is less difficult when we know God is omniscient and He is the only one who has the right to seek revenge. In Biblical times people carried burning coals on their heads to light fires for cooking and heating. So, giving someone burning coals was helping them, not hurting them. However, don't think that when you have been wronged, God will lower the boom on that person. Even if you have been afflicted by the world's standards more than the Lord's, He will seek vengeance in His own time and possibly in a way you may not like. God also is patient and loving. He desires for people to seek repentance and come back to Him. Think about how many of us would be left on earth if God was like us. *You cheated on me! Zap! You lied about me! Zap!* We laugh because we know it is true.

You never know how God is dealing with a person behind the scenes. We may think they have gotten away with it and are living great lives, but we never know the heartbreak and disappointment or the conviction and misery that God is bringing into their lives. The Lord has a whole arsenal—everything in the world—and He is all-powerful. God can do anything. So, never give up hoping a situation will turn around. Live the way you know God wants you to live, and let him take care of the situation.

One day, when I was teaching in the jail, I was talking to the women about forgiving those who have hurt you and not seeking revenge. A woman came up to me afterward and said, "I wish I had heard this years ago." Curious, I looked her up when I got home. She had hired someone to kill her ex-husband. Fortunately for him, the person she hired was an undercover officer. She was looking at a lot of prison time. Sad stories like this are quite common. Even though she divorced her husband, she allowed bitterness and anger to continue in her life. Instead of seeking counseling and learning to cope with the hurt and disappointment, she continued letting the hurt fester until she decided to have him killed. Now, she was coming face to face with life in prison. Her career, her hopes and dreams for the, future, and most importantly, her freedom were all gone. Deciding to seek revenge can destroy your life. Seek help and know that actions begin in the mind.

As you muse on the principles in this book, keep in mind that many people know the scriptures but do not apply them to their daily lives. James is a great book to read and learn the basics of controlling your tongue and guarding your life. "For if any be a hearer of the word, and not a doer, he is like unto a man beholding his natural face in a glass: For he beholdeth himself, and goeth his way and straightway forgetteth what manner of man he was. But whoso looketh into the perfect law of liberty, and continueth therein, he being not a forgetful hearer, but a doer of the work, this man shall be blessed in his deed. If any man among you seem to be religious, and bridleth not his tongue, but deceiveth his own heart, this man's religion is vain." (James 1:23–26, KJV)

It is not the readings that bless your life but the application of the readings. People will see *a new you* and will wonder what happened to you. What a witnessing opportunity! Earlier this week, I was watching the incredible movie *Amazing Grace*. It is the true story of how William Wilberforce fought and eventually was able to get England out of the slave trade. His pastor, John Newton, a former slave ship captain, wrote the song *Amazing Grace* after accepting the Lord as His Savior and leaving the slave trade. In my opinion, the greatest line in the movie is when John Newton says to Wilberforce, "All I know is that I am a great sinner and Christ is a great Savior."

By accepting the Lord and looking into the scriptures, Newton saw his grievous sin and recognized the vast forgiveness he received in Jesus Christ. That is what I strive for in my life, that all of us will see that we are great sinners and what a great Savior we have in Christ!

The Lord wants to give us abundant life in Him. We can have that through yielding ourselves to the Holy Spirit daily and letting Him change our lives so we can be like Christ and draw all men to Him. What a privilege we have as believers! Someday, we will be with Christ in eternity and join the people that we helped bring to Him throughout our lives.